BOASTING IN WEAKNESS

BOASTING IN WEAKNESS

OVERCOMING SELF-RELIANCE, PERFECTION, AND SUPERIORITY

RICK THOMAS

BOASTING IN WEAKNESS:
Overcoming Self-Reliance, Perfection, and Superiority

ISBN 978-1-7323854-6-7

Rick Thomas

© 2025 Life Over Coffee

Unless otherwise noted, all Scripture references herein are from the English Standard Version, copyright © 2001 by Crossway, Inc. Used by permission. All rights reserved.

No part of this publication may be reproduced, stored in a retrieval system, or transmitted in any form or by any means without the express written permission of Life Over Coffee.

Edited by Sarah Hayhurst

Life Over Coffee
8595 Pelham Rd Ste 400 #406,
Greenville, SC 29615
LifeOverCoffee.com

Therefore I will boast all the more gladly of my
weaknesses, so that the power of Christ
may rest upon me.
(2 Corinthians 12:9)

For additional resources, visit
lifeovercoffee.com

Table of Contents

    Introduction 8
1. Jars of Clay 14
2. Boasting 24
3. Unguarded Strength 32
4. Standard Lowering 40
5. Perfect Problems 48
6. Perfect Praise 56
7. Need to Die 64
8. Beyond Your Ability 72
9. Comfort Zones 82
10. Self-reliance 90
    About the Author 100

Introduction

The situational difficulties we face are the contexts that reveal our hearts, which is how God purifies our faith and obedience. These personal, relational, and situational challenges are our opportunities to follow Jesus in the Christian's call to suffer well. Paul discussed it as boasting in his weakness, but what does that mean? I want to take you on a journey through the New Testament, laying out how God chooses life's foolish and weak things to confound the wise. Every dinged and dented jar of clay that God uses understands this "boasting in weakness worldview," but for many of our brothers and sisters, it continues to be a mental challenge to shift from their former manner of life to putting on Christ (Ephesians 4:22–23).

The Fearful Call

Though a call to suffer does not bode well in our evangelistic endeavors, it's vital to inform all those interested in the gospel that there are two—not one—gifts that God gives each person at the point of their regeneration. The first blessed package to unwrap is salvation, and the second is the gift of suffering. Paul said it this way:

> For it has been granted to you that for the sake of Christ you should not only believe in him but also suffer for his sake.
>
> (Philippians 1:29)

Introduction

This second gift can be such a problem in the believer's life that it hinders their growth in Christ. The average believer has an inadequate theology of suffering. If you asked them about this call from God, they might stammer to articulate the query while quizzically staring as they wrestle with the terminology. The irony is that suffering is not to make our lives miserable but to teach us to trust the Lord rather than rely on ourselves. Self-reliance—a form of unbelief—is our biggest nemesis.

> Although he was a son, he learned obedience through what he suffered. And being made perfect, he became the source of eternal salvation to all who obey him.
> (Hebrews 5:8-9)

> For we do not want you to be unaware, brothers, of the affliction we experienced in Asia. For we were so utterly burdened beyond our strength that we despaired of life itself. Indeed, we felt that we had received the sentence of death. But that was to make us rely not on ourselves but on God who raises the dead.
> (2 Corinthians 1:8-9)

This anti-modern message that promotes weakness as the pathway to power teaches us to die to ourselves (Luke 9:23; Galatians 2:20). It is one of the primary means of grace the Lord provides to create an other-worldly reliance on the only legit superpower. Though the message of death is unnerving at first glance, there are many biblical precedents, including God's intentional crushing of His Son, as we learn in Isaiah.

> Yet it was the will of the Lord to crush him; he has put him to grief.
> (Isaiah 53:10)

Our Call to Suffer

Occasionally, people will ask me to help them understand God's call on their life. While I do not know all that the Lord has in mind for them, I do know He has called every Christian to suffer well. Peter could not be more explicit about this matter.

> Servants, be subject to your masters with all respect, not only to the good and gentle but also to the unjust. For this is a gracious thing, when, mindful of God, one endures sorrows while suffering unjustly. For what credit is it if, when you sin and are beaten for it, you endure? But if when you do good and suffer for it you endure, this is a gracious thing in the sight of God. For to this, you have been called, because Christ also suffered for you, leaving you an example, so that you might follow in his steps.
> (1 Peter 2:18–21)

The Steps of Jesus

If we are to walk in the steps of Jesus, the question becomes, what are those steps? What did Jesus do? Let's look at how Peter articulated the steps of the Savior in this passage that lays out our calling.

- He did not sin.
- There was no deceit in His mouth.
- When individuals reviled Him, He did not revile in return.
- When He suffered, He did not threaten.
- He always entrusted Himself to Him who judges justly.

> He himself bore our sins in his body on the tree, that we might die to sin and live to righteousness.

> *By his wounds, you have been healed. For you were straying like sheep, but have now returned to the Shepherd and Overseer of your souls.*
>
> (1 Peter 2:24–25)

Granted, we will not save anyone as Jesus does, but God calls us to walk in His steps, which anyone can see is a path of suffering. The quick-thinking believer will say, "But He was Jesus, and I'm not Him." True enough. The good news is that God has given us a backup plan when we fail to hit the high mark of suffering like Jesus. You can confess those failures while continuing His death march (1 John 1:9). Only Christians can repent, making it one of our high-powered secret weapons. Imagine having a way to clean up your messes!

Suffering and Relationships

Interestingly, Peter put his suffering passage just before his marriage passage and joined the two sections with the conjunction likewise so we would know they are connected. How cool is that? His point is clear: if you don't have the correct view of suffering, you cannot live well with your spouse—or anyone else. Without a sound theology of suffering, you will likely sin against your spouse the first time he or she does not meet your expectations. A sinful response to a failing spouse is the exact opposite of how Christ responds to us when we fail (John 3:16; Romans 5:8; Matthew 18:35). I cannot overstate the need for sound theology and a biblical application of suffering.

> *Likewise, wives, be subject to your own husbands, so that even if some do not obey the word, they may be won without a word by the conduct of their wives, when they see your respectful and pure conduct. Do not let your adorning be external—the braiding*

> of hair and the putting on of gold jewelry, or the clothing you wear—but let your adorning be the hidden person of the heart with the imperishable beauty of a gentle and quiet spirit, which in God's sight is very precious. Likewise, husbands, live with your wives in an understanding way, showing honor to the woman as the weaker vessel, since they are heirs with you of the grace of life, so that your prayers may not be hindered.
>
> (1 Peter 3:1-7)

Purpose of Suffering

Could it be, like Paul, that the good Lord brings specific individuals or circumstances into our lives so we can learn the obedience that the Hebrew writer talked about? (Hebrews 5:8—He learned obedience through what He suffered.) Learning obedience was, without question, the purpose of Paul's suffering. He tells us all about it at the end of 2 Corinthians.

> So to keep me from becoming conceited because of the surpassing greatness of the revelations, a thorn was given me in the flesh, a messenger of Satan to harass me, to keep me from becoming conceited. Three times I pleaded with the Lord about this, that it should leave me. But he said to me, "My grace is sufficient for you, for my power is made perfect in weakness." Therefore I will boast all the more gladly of my weaknesses, so that the power of Christ may rest upon me. For the sake of Christ, then, I am content with weaknesses, insults, hardships, persecutions, and calamities. For when I am weak, then I am strong.
>
> (2 Corinthians 12:7-10)

Paul learned the secret to life when he said that his weakness was the condition that brought God's strength to him, which helps us to understand why he was boasting in his weakness. Vulnerability and fragility are not something to resist because God will only place His surpassing power into such fragile clay vessels (2 Corinthians 4:7; Genesis 2:7). The question for us to entertain is whether we want to assume the position of weakness, vulnerability, and fragility to experience the wonder-working power of God operating through us.

Call to Action

1. How would you describe your practical understanding of suffering? I'm calling it a theology of suffering. Based on your reading, would you share your view of suffering with a friend?
2. Do you need to change your view of suffering so you can learn obedience through your relational or situational challenges? If so, what is your specific and practical plan to start that process?
3. Have you found strength in your weakness like Paul, or do you resist the weakness that suffering brings into our lives? What does your answer reveal about you and God? If you should address something, will you create a transformation plan?
4. Will you share with a friend your thoughts about boasting in your weakness? What does that phrase mean? How does it encourage you? What does it reveal about God's method for empowering His children?

1

Jars of Clay

A cracked jar of clay does not have to be a bad thing if you know the Potter. God prefers His creation to be fragile jars of clay, so He can display His miraculous, surpassing power to our friends and the culture. Of course, there is a problem with this perspective. Adamic clay pots are not content being fragile, vulnerable, or weak. We envy strength, power, might, and other self-reliant strategies for self-protection and, sometimes, self-promotion. This counterintuitive message about the gospel cuts against the grain of proud hearts.

Unusual Ways

In 2 Corinthians 4:7–12, we learn how Paul thought about the power through weakness message. He was afflicted, and it was as though it did not matter which way he turned; someone was always persecuting him. To find trouble was to find Paul. Paul and trouble were like two peas in a pod. According to him, he experienced affliction in every way. Paul was perplexed, persecuted, and pushed down. He was always carrying in his body the death of Jesus—bringing us to a most crucial and practical question. How about you? How goes it? How's your day, your week, your life? Are you experiencing affliction? Have you had seasons where things did not go your way?

Let me venture a guess here: you have. How do I know

this? Because you are a human—a fragile jar of clay. You're a disposable pot. How about this twist: though times of affliction are some of the more undesirable seasons in anyone's life, it is precisely in those moments when God receives His most wondrous glory, and we experience other-worldly power. Of course, this perspective raises more questions, at least to me: Do I want my affliction to be a means to glorify God? Better yet, do I want to be afflicted at all? What if I continue to rely on myself rather than Him who raises the dead (2 Corinthians 1:8–9)?

I remember vividly unique seasons in my life when I was afflicted, and God's glory was not at the top of my list of hopeful outcomes. My primary aim was to escape the traumatic time. However, if I were honest, I would say it was in those moments of despair that I experienced God in incredible and unusual ways. The people I served during those seasons experienced God's help through this broken jar of clay in ways I could not conjure through mere human intellect. Only afterward do I have such sovereign clarity. I'm confident you've had those moments too.

Death and Life

There is a tension here; I am not looking to suffer, but I know that my suffering magnifies the fame of God and empowers me in other-worldly ways. It is also true that nothing will objectively measure my Christian maturity more than when I am in times of personal difficulty. Though I can fake you out sometimes, I cannot always fake you out, and personal affliction is one of those times when the real me comes out, whether for the good or the bad. To know the real me is to understand me when I'm afflicted, bringing us to the best news of all!

I do not have to despair. There is always hope for the Christian. The good news is that God will not leave me alone in my affliction. God is in my suffering, always working His good purposes through this weak and fragile piece of clay. Few passages in the Bible break down God's comprehensive help for the believer more clearly than 2 Corinthians 4:7–12. Paul gives us one of his most profound gospel-centered perspectives on afflictions in this passage.

> But we have this treasure in jars of clay, to show that the surpassing power belongs to God and not to us. We are afflicted in every way, but not crushed; perplexed, but not driven to despair; persecuted, but not forsaken; struck down but not destroyed; always carrying in the body the death of Jesus, so that the life of Jesus may also be manifested in our bodies. For we who live are always being given over to death for Jesus' sake, so that the life of Jesus also may be manifested in our mortal flesh. So death is at work in us, but life in you.
>
> (2 Corinthians 4:7–12)

Disposable Houses

> We have this treasure in jars of clay.
>
> —Paul

I think sometimes I can forget that my body is decaying and disposable. Though the gospel is evident, teaching me that I am a dying man, I can drift from this truth, thinking my life and creature comforts are more important than the life God is calling me to. Honestly, the container I live in is not all that important; it should never receive precedence in my heart. But what is in my container is the thing that is important and the thing that matters most. Whenever I put too much emphasis on my container rather than the content of the container, the temptation is to lose heart. I can despair.

> We are afflicted in every way but not crushed, perplexed but not driven to despair.
>
> —Paul

When I do not see myself as a pilgrim passing through this wilderness land, I can succumb to the temptation to savor the life I live more than the purposes of God, the One who is writing His story into the life that I am living. Perhaps framing the question this way will help: am I more interested in and fixated on the container or the content in the container? Which is it for you? What occupies more of your mental time and emotional space? Problem-centered people will focus more on and talk more about the problems in their lives. Christ-centered people will focus more on how to put Christ on display through the circumstances in their lives.

Suffering does not deny the gospel but confirms the gospel. From Paul's perspective, he did not see suffering as what should dominate his mental space or conversation. He understood that life in a clay world was destined for failure, brokenness, and deterioration. He got that. It's like lamenting growing old, turning gray, or experiencing increased diminishing capacities. These things are who we are as clay pots. Dying is what we do. We are jars of clay that God did not build to last. Because of the fall of Adam, we die, suffer affliction, and experience nicks, dings, brokenness, and damage.

Accepting Weakness

> For we who live are always being given over to death for Jesus' sake so that the life of Jesus also may be manifested in our mortal flesh.
>
> —Paul

The issue should never be primarily about what is happening to us—regarding our afflictions. God made us weak and fragile. Fragile things are always afflicted. The real deal is that we are vulnerable and moldable clay pots that God wants to inhabit. This mystery about our clay-ness raises a question and points to a secret: why would God make something so weak and fragile? By design, God entrusts this secret about His glory and our mysterious strength to failing, wounded, vulnerable, and sinful people, so it will be apparent that the power does not originate from us. It doesn't result from a strong personality, keen, finely honed mind, or good breeding or training. No, it arises solely from the presence of God in our hearts.

> Our earthiness must be as apparent to others as the power is so that they see that the secret is not us but God. We must be a transparent people, not hiding our weaknesses and failures, but honestly admitting them when they occur.
>
> —Ray Stedman

God has always intended for us to be jars of clay, which contain the treasure of His glory for us to put on display, but be warned: God will not compete with us. It will either be our strength or His strength, but it will never be our strength and His strength. To magnify His power, He created us in breakable, disposable, weak, and fragile clay pots. It's not about the pot but about what is in the pot. If you could accept that you are weak, broken, and damaged, you would begin to see and experience God working in you, bringing about His glory to others.

Gospel Paradox

> We are afflicted in every way but not crushed; perplexed but not driven to despair; persecuted but not forsaken; struck down but not destroyed.
>
> —Paul

We are jars of clay, called to put the gospel on display through our brokenness. Notice the paradox in Paul's theology of suffering.

- On the one hand, we are afflicted, but on the other hand, we are not crushed.
- On the one hand, we are perplexed, but on the other hand, we are not driven to despair.
- On the one hand, we are persecuted, but on the other hand, we are not forsaken.
- On the one hand, we are struck down, but on the other hand, we are not destroyed.

It takes a paradox to put God on display; it takes a clay pot, and it takes God's power in the pot. Though you will experience affliction, you will not experience terminal crushing. Though there will be perplexing times, God's grace will keep you from utter despair. Though there will be persecution, the good Lord will never leave or forsake you. Guard your heart. Your affliction is not primarily about something you did wrong or what someone did to you. It's about God working in you.

Sovereign God is always working, always on the job, and always helping you to put His name on display. God's primary work is what affliction is about in your life. Your or someone else's challenges are merely how God's name goes on display. Guard your heart against the temptation of bitterness when thinking about affliction, especially how your affliction came to you. God is with you. God is working in you. This suffering worldview is a life-shaping, trajectory-altering, gospel-centered, grace-motivating truth.

Do You Believe?

> *For we who live are always being given over to death for Jesus' sake so that the life of Jesus also may be manifested in our mortal flesh. So death is at work in us, but life in you.*
>
> —Paul

The difference between experiencing affliction, perplexity, and being struck down but not being crushed, driven to despair, and destroyed, is how you understand and live out the power of the gospel. Believing the gospel is different than being willing to live according to how the gospel is supposed to work in you. Experiencing the life of Jesus comes by embracing the death of Jesus. The suffering Paul experienced was so that people could see the gospel through his broken jar. While he was experiencing the death of Christ in his mortal body, he saw the life of Jesus manifested in the lives of others.

How often have you seen Christ's life manifested through Christ's death? If you have seen or experienced this, you know it only happened because God worked in and through a broken jar of clay. I have heard many testimonies about men and women who went through suffering and how, through their suffering, they shared the life of Christ with others. Sometimes God will put you in places that feel like death, but if you embrace these things by faith, the life of Jesus will come through your brokenness.

Paul's faith in the gospel kept him from losing heart. He would suffer more if he could only manifest Christ's life to others. What Paul wanted for himself and others was a practical experience of the gospel: Christ took on death so we could have life. Living like Christ means living with weakness, challenges, and difficulties while dying to self for the sake of others. Of course, this experience happens daily, bringing us to some counterintuitive news: the more deaths you die, the more you will display Christ's life for others, and the more God will be glorified.

Life Implies Death

Truly, truly, I say to you, unless a grain of wheat falls into the earth and dies, it remains alone; but if it dies, it bears much fruit.

(John 12:24)

There is no way around this big truth: if you want to live, you must die. Out of death comes life. Out of weakness comes strength. Out of jars of clay comes the power of God. The suffering you experience today is not a denial of the gospel but a confirmation of the gospel. Living the gospel life is what this life is all about, and it is the only way to live this life for God's glory. When you willingly choose to take on the death of Jesus, the strangest thing will happen; you will display the life of Jesus. How can you die today? How is God calling you to put Christ on display? Perhaps you need to reconcile with your spouse, even though you're not the primary one who is guilty. Is God calling you to die to your expectations, rights, and preferences for greater glory—His glory put on display through you?

Maybe you are a teenage son or daughter walking waywardly from God and your parents. Is God calling you to die to your anger, to take on the death of Christ so that you can demonstrate His life through you? Believe this: no matter what affliction you are going through, God promises that if you willingly embrace the death of what is happening to you and turn your heart toward this kind of gospel worldview, you will not be crushed, driven to despair, forsaken, or destroyed. Yes, you will experience death, but the life of Christ will shine out of your broken jar of clay.

Call to Action

1. Will you believe the gospel today, the functional, practical gospel? What does that question mean to you? How would you practically apply the gospel—death and life of Christ—to your life today?
2. In what way do you struggle with being a fragile jar of clay? What does your struggle reveal about your theology of suffering? What specific way do you need to change, and what is your plan?
3. Who do you know that is struggling as a jar of clay? Assuming you have the relational bridge, context, and time to encourage them, will you ask the Father to provide the grace and act upon it by going to that person to care for them?

Jars of Clay

2

Boasting

Boasting in your weakness is a strange juxtaposition of words. Typically, you don't connect boasting with weakness unless you mock someone about their inability to accomplish a feat. We call it bullying. But in God's economy, boasting is something every Christian should do as they think about being weak, vulnerable, and fragile because mature believers know that God will not compete with them. It can't be strength and strength but weakness and strength. We see this concept in the death of Christ, causing the disciples to struggle to wrap their minds around the counterintuitive gospel message.

Pot Pressure

In 2 Corinthians 12:1-10, Paul clearly and transparently lays out his reasons for boasting in his weaknesses. We call it the thorn in the flesh passage where he plainly said that he would boast in his weakness so the power of Christ would rest on him. The more you understand that section of God's Word, the more you'll be able to comprehend the purpose of suffering and how God perfects His strength in our weaknesses. Similar to the clay pot in 2 Corinthians 4:7, where Paul implied we must accept that we are jars of Adamic clay. The most significant stumbling block for anyone to grasp this message is our former manner of life—that time we spent as non-believers, receiving the cultural indoctrination that became our primary shaping influences. Here are a few typical examples of how our former manner of life becomes a deterrent to counterintuitive gospel thinking.

- Fathers pressure their children to be their best, striving to improve, creating a competitive spirit in the child where winning is the only thing.
- Fear of others lures the insecure soul to compare themselves with others, hoping nobody will notice their weakness and mock them for not meeting the standard.
- The culture applauds winners and frowns on losers so much that they change the rules so everyone can win and not suffer the embarrassment of not measuring up.
- The Hollywood elites tell us what beauty and perfection are, and too many women are insecure enough to accept the gaslighting, transforming themselves into cultural norms.
- Of course, the sports world is rife with discontented athletes as their glory fades, and the star is the last to accept reality, so he retires, un-retires, and retires again.

He does not know how to rejoice in his weaknesses. Somebody coached him up since Pop Warner, instilling a mindset that he's the greatest. His strength unleashed became the zeitgeist that stirred an insatiable desire to compete and conquer. The hard truth is that we are similar to the glory-seeking athlete. Discontentment and insecurity easily entangle us, creating a disdain for being weak, average, different, insecure, fallen, imperfect, homely, unsuccessful, or rejected. Pick your poison; we all struggle similarly. It is hard for a clay pot to accept that being disposable, not good enough, or not immortal enough is the best we can be. Ask the superstar. Ask the average guy who is embarrassed about his career path or the average woman who is overly self-aware of the advancement of old age.

Broken Pots

The nature of the jar of clay implies imperfection, but the proud heart and the discontented soul will have difficulty accepting this truth. I saw a bumper sticker that said, "My kid belongs to the no cavity club." Really? I immediately thought about making a bumper sticker that said, "My kid is a B student with three cavities." The craving heart will always be on the prowl for significance, even if it's in his bicuspid. (I'm not knocking healthy teeth but saying the unguarded door of crouching pride always seeks to devour the high-minded.) If you think this is not a significant problem, I recommend spending time with abortion advocates or euthanasia proponents.

There is an innate, insidious Adamic reason they want to kill people. Weakness and deformity are contrary to the self-reliant spirit of our age. Though the death proponents are some of the more outlandish illustrations of people who hate weakness, we are not significantly different because we have an internal disdain for the death in our bodies. We were born to break, born to die. Deterioration is part of what the curse means. God built us to last, but Adam sinned, and everything took on the smell of death. The Lord condemned us to die (Genesis 2:16–17), though His mercy would not allow us to be trapped in a body of death forever.

Thus, the deteriorating effect of sin begins at birth. A self-aware fallen pot intuits the death march, and pursues self-reliant strategies to resist fallenness, not realizing soon enough that any joy outside of God's strength is hollow. Living in God's reality is where genuine joy begins. Rejoicing in our weakness is recognizing and accepting that our fallenness is the proper starting place. We must determine that we will not succumb to discouragement as we consider our disposable-ness. As Christian pots, we must press into the greater truths of the gospel. A sanctified pot does not sit around, lamenting that it's dirty, disposable, rejected, and undesirable.

Happy Pots

The pot has a bigger vision than the squalidness of their former manner of life (Ephesians 4:17–22). Like Paul Harvey used to tell us, "Now, for the rest of the story." The pot is on the road to rejoicing in its weakness because the pot knows it's not stuck in the rut of its weakness. He knows that only through weakness-thinking and application that the power of Christ will manifest in its life. The pot's weakness has a higher purpose. Paul said it this way: "We have this treasure in jars of clay to show that the surpassing power belongs to God and not to us" (2 Corinthians 4:7). Are you discouraged because you are a clay pot? Do you wish you were not the way you are? Does the way some people treat you discourage you? Are you a pot shaped by other individuals? There are at least three reasons clay pots become angry:

- They dislike how God made them.
- They don't like the way others have shaped them.
- They don't like a combination of both: what God did to them and what others did to them.

If you are a frustrated pot because of how you are, you cannot experience genuine joy until you change your mind. You'll need to accept your pot identity to become a happy pot. Jesus did not come for pretty pots. Pretty pots do not need His assistance. He looks for the fragile, dinged, dented, and downcast pot. Jesus came for that person who owns his fallenness, recognizes that he can't do anything about it, and seeks Christ. Did you know it is hard for some people to talk about their sins or let others know they have failed in particular ways? It's true. Many individuals in the Christian community hide behind a wall of fear of being exposed. They are shame-filled and sin-focused.

Though these fearful people don't publicly talk about their sins—to the proper and appropriate friends, they know something is wrong with themselves. It is hard for them to accept who they are, so they won't talk about who they are to the proper people: they don't want anyone to know. Because of this fear of being found out or their frustration with being a jar, they indulge in self-pity or choose anger. Acceptance does not mean you can never change or enjoy your broken condition. Acceptance is acknowledging. It means being honest, open, transparent, and humble about yourself. Calvary is blaring into our psyche that we are a broken people. Our consciences are also shouting at us, reminding us of who we are. Fallenness is only a bad thing for the self-righteous person who disdains exposure.

Knowing the Potter

Embracing fallenness is why the Pharisees had such a hard time accepting the gospel's truth: they were weak, fallen, inadequate, moral failures, and in need of Christ. Rather than accepting reality and Christ, they created a system for overcoming their weaknesses. Manufactured strategies to do all things through themselves are at the heart of self-reliance—half-measures that will end poorly for its participants (Philippians 4:13). A high-minded clay pot shudders to think they can be a bad, broken-down, and disposable clay pot. On their worst days, they sink into self-pity with dark reminders that crave hope and desire to be better than what their fallenness pronounces them to be.

If this is where you go in your heart when you think about your inadequacies, you will never be able to get on the path of boasting in your weaknesses. This juncture is where you must take your soul to task, reminding yourself that when you break, get dinged, or chip, those things will not ultimately cast you down or destroy you (Psalm 42:5-6; 2 Corinthians 4:7-10). Of course, if no one could fix a broken clay pot, there would be no reason to rejoice. Fortunately, for the Christian, there is not only acknowledgment and acceptance of fallenness but an awareness of the one who made the pot and His ability to overcome fallenness through the power of His gospel. Even in his weaknesses, the clay pot can rejoice because he knows that utter destruction will never be his portion.

Something profound and other-worldly happens because of our connection with the Potter. It's like a little boy standing before his daddy while being accused or verbally assaulted by another boy on the playground. He is not hung up or overly focused on his inferiorities, insecurities, or inadequacies because he knows his daddy is with him (Matthew 28:20). Contrariwise, the self-righteous clay pot will never be content with the fragileness of the moment. The self-righteous boy will constantly lament that he can't whoop the other kid, was made fun of or put down, or does not measure up in some way. He will always long to be better, superior, robust, or profound. It does not matter that his daddy is there.

Rejoicing in Weakness

What should happen is that he should focus on what his daddy can do because of the boy's weaknesses or despite his weaknesses. The boy with a high view of himself will never be satisfied, content, or at rest. He will always be striving to be stronger, bigger, and better. Each time he fails, he will plummet into more misery, never realizing or acknowledging that his daddy is there to rescue him. He will spin in a sin cycle by not relying on God's strength. He will be frustrated because he can't be better than he is. If the little boy begins to understand and apply the gospel, he will become more content with who he is, a simple ding-able clay pot.

He will focus less on what he has or does not have while rejoicing in what God can do through him. Boasting in our weaknesses is accepting the facts of our fallenness while clinging to our strong Savior. It is not a zip-a-dee-doo-dah, I have sinned attitude, but a combination of these truths:

> *I will never be anything more than a clay pot on earth. I'm inadequate in my strengths. I don't have to strive to be something I am not. God made me the way I am so that His surpassing power can work in and through me. When His strength works through me, it glorifies God, and I live in His immense pleasure's goodness.*

Therefore, we have a steady and consistent heart of gratitude; we rejoice in our weaknesses. If it were not for our weaknesses, the power of Christ could not be in us or work through us, the cause of our rejoicing. We must accept our weaknesses while cooperating with God's strength that He is perfecting in us. Our rejoicing is not because of sin. It is because of the combination and the accumulative effect of having a treasure in a jar of clay. It's like saying,

> Yes, I am weak, but you must know who my daddy is. He's the One who can do great and mighty things through my weakness that will blow your mind. And in this, I rejoice.

Call to Action

1. What does it mean to boast in your weakness? Will you carve out some time soon to talk with a friend, explaining this concept of boasting in your weakness?
2. How has the indoctrination of the culture hindered or prohibited you from accepting your weaknesses?
3. What are the top two things that make boasting in your weakness hard for you to live out practically?
4. Is there at least one person who knows the real you? Our temptation is to self-edit ourselves and promote that person while hiding our shame-ridden selves.
5. Perhaps you have a friend who lives behind a mask—fig leaves; they sense the shame that weakens them. What would you like to say to them, hoping to get them to see that boasting in weakness is a worldview that transforms lives?

3

Unguarded Strength

An unguarded strength is a double weakness. After all, we rarely guard our strengths because we think of them as good, not realizing that our abilities can entrap us, keeping us from relying on God. Let me illustrate my point with a counseling session with a mother and daughter. The child's strength was her intellect, propelling her to do well in school. The unguardedness of her skills created a darkness in the child's life that brought them to counseling. If we are not wise in stewarding our strengths, we can become blind too.

Family Affair

Mable came to counseling to talk about her daughter, Biffina. Biffina is thirteen years old and has been acting out recently. It has been chiefly anger and a sassy attitude toward her parents and little brother, Biffy. She added that Biffina had not been eating and may be struggling there too. Her mom noted how her anger had escalated over the past year, and she did not know what to do about it. She talked to her husband, Biff, as well as her teachers. Typically, when a mom or dad comes to me for counseling regarding one of their children, there are some specific questions I need to ask the parents—about the parents.

A thirteen-year-old child does not typically become as rebellious as Mable described regarding their daughter without assistance. In most cases of teen rebellion, this is more than just a child problem. I reject the cultural lie that says the teen years are predetermined to be years of rebellion and that you can do nothing about it. Christians can factor in the gospel's transformative power into people's lives, which is the perfect antidote for rebellion, regardless of age. Though there are exceptions in that some children rebel without the adverse shaping influences of their parents, more times than not, there are things the parents have been doing that facilitated the teen's rebellion.

As things turned out for Biffina, there were some specific things Mable and Biff could have done differently. In this case, it was a kid's problem and a parents' problem. The interesting thing about this situation was that Mable knew it was a parent issue but would not admit it at the beginning of our counseling session. She presented the case as though it was all about Biffina, and what they needed to do about it baffled them. Ultimately, Mable did not want to tell me how her husband was a significant culprit in Biffina's rebellion because Mable felt hopeless that Biff would ever change. Rather than being honest with me about the situation, she presented it as teen rebellion and wanted me to fix their daughter.

Data-gathering

Counseling was a last-ditch effort for a mom who fell between a rock and a hard place. She could not change her husband, so she hoped that she could hire me to fix their broken daughter. I understood her hopelessness, but Mable could not skirt the parenting problem if she wanted restoration. Biff was part of Biffina's problem, and as long as he was unchanging, it would have a distinguishable impact on how Biffina chose to live through her teenage years. It is like trying to lose weight while stuffing down a six-pack of soda and three Snickers bars a day. You cannot maintain the wrong behavior and expect a different result.

Biff and Mable could not continue in their habits and hope that Biffina changes magically. The intent of counseling was never to do what Mable wanted it to do. If the grace of God were to intervene mercifully, it would be within the scope of God's domain and prerogative, not mine. God's grace can overcome our foolishness, but we should never presume on His grace to do that (Psalm 19:13). With this re-clarification in view, I began asking Mable some specific questions: "You talked to her teachers; what did they say?" Mable told me that Biffina's teachers were surprised that she was rebellious. Their perception of Biffina was that she was a model child.

Mable talked to six of her teachers from this year's class and some of her previous teachers. All six of them, past and present, had similar stories: Biffina is a wonderfully compliant child. She has never caused a minute's trouble and is an academic example to all her classmates. The real truth about Biffina is that she is rebellious in every area except school. The school is the only place where she is a model child. This information was helpful on several fronts. First of all, it told me that Biffina could behave. There were some character issues in play rather than physical limitations. Biffina could be nice if she wanted to be, and she could misbehave if she wanted to. She had the moral ability to choose right or wrong behaviors.

Desiring Love

"What does your parenting model look like in your home?" I asked. Mable told me that she spends most of her time with Biffina, while Biff spends most of his time with Biffy. Mable was unsure why it was that way, but that is how they have always done it. During this part of the conversation,

Mable told me that Biffina asked her when she was four or five years old, "Mommy, why does Daddy play with Biffy and does not play with me?" The effects of their parenting stirred an instructive question from little Biffina. She was struggling with a situation that would soon set the trajectory for the rest of her life, though she did not know it then or now.

Mable did not perceive the significance of Biffina's question about her daddy, though she was beginning to understand now what Biffina had been harboring in her heart all these years. What does Biff's relationship with Biffina lack? Mable said Biff rarely encourages his daughter. Though their home is not overly hostile or discouraging, it is not where active and intentional building up and encouragement occurs. After chatting with Biffina, it became apparent that affection and attention from her daddy were paramount. From her perspective, Biff seemed preoccupied, disinterested, and distant. At times, he even came across as angry, according to Biffina.

Biffina assumed as a young child that Biffy would be okay if something terrible happened to their family. He would be safe, but she was not as confident daddy would protect her. When I finally met with Biffina, I asked her, during a long conversation and many questions, "Biffina, what are you more aware of: your daddy's correction and displeasure or your daddy's affection and encouragement?" It was incredible. Biffina's eyes began to water immediately. She had already figured it out: "Daddy loves Biffy, but he does not love me." Her dad's lack of affection for her created confusion in her heart. It was a setup for personal failure. The results of their parenting also explained why she was so angry.

Father Pictures

Then she hesitated but finally murmured that her daddy rarely encouraged her and that she always felt he was displeased with her. She did clarify how many times it was not necessarily because of what he said as much as it was about his quietness, distance, preoccupation, and obvious affection for Biffy. The church was one of the many contexts where Biffina was rebellious. She disdained church. The parents' response to her hatred of religion was to press the issue. They saw it as another aspect of her rebellion they could change through force. Sadly, they were not discerning the problem.

Biffina rebelled because it was her way of working through her struggle with God. She did not know how to have a relationship with God because the primary authority figure in her life—her father—demotivated her to want to have a relationship with another father. Biffina felt her dad's displeasure and naturally assumed God's anger. "If Daddy does not like me, God must not like me either. There must be something wrong with me." Biffina believed God was angry with her. From her perspective, it was like being thrown in a room with an angry person, so Biffina became angry too. She said God seemed distant, and Biffina did not know where she stood with the Lord.

Though she believed God had saved her when she was nine, there was still this inward, awkward nagging and uncertainty about her relationship with God. Biffina said that she needed to perform for God to stand well with Him. Though she knew her thinking was incorrect, there was still this yearning in her heart to do right to be accepted by God. When I began to talk to Biffina about her school, I noticed an almost immediate change in her disposition. She perked up and was glad to tell me about her straight A's. She told me three times in five minutes that she was an A student. One of the things her mother said to me was that Biffina learned in Kindergarten that she was brilliant. Shortly after entering Kindergarten, Biffina found her niche. Biffina had a gift, and that gift was her intelligence.

Unguarded Strength

When Biffina began turning in her papers to her first-grade teacher, the papers would come back with stars and smiley faces at the top of them. How Biffina felt in those moments of getting her papers back was something she rarely felt at any time in her life. Biffina felt appreciated. She felt loved. She felt approved. Biffina had a God-given strength, which was her intelligence, and she learned how her intelligence would be the gateway to many good things, especially love and significance. I asked Biffina about her excellent grades and what they meant to her.

She said, "Daddy told me a long time ago the best way I could make him happy was to make all A's. Daddy doesn't care for the lack of effort, particularly in school. He said he did not try hard in school, which was his worst mistake. He does not want me to do poorly in school." Biffina took his warning to heart; from her perspective, she saw it as fortunate to be a bright girl. Biffina saw it as a gift, though it blinded her to how her greatest strength was also her biggest weakness. The raw truth was that neither she nor her father and mother could see how her pursuit of good grades and excellence through education was idolatry.

Biffina was an idolater, and her daddy was one of the culprits pushing her deeper into her idolatry. The more we talked, the more open Biffina became. She eventually shared with me how she cheated on a test on one occasion last year. I was the first person she ever let in on her secret. Biffina was so hungry for attention from her dad that she rationalized the cheating. Her guilt-ridden conscience had eaten away at her for over a year, but her craving for love was more significant than her temptation to sin. Her guilty conscience was another reason she had an aggravated relationship with God and almost everyone else. She was getting the love she craved through academic success, but in her heart of hearts, Biffina knew she was getting her fix on at a high price. Her frustration mounted.

A Little Idolator

To make matters worse, the unresolved guilt in her conscience began to work out in bad eating habits. She could not tell anyone what she had done, but Biffina knew there had to be some punishment for her sin, so she punished herself. As you break down her logic, it went along these lines. Dad was distant, so she could not tell him. God was displeased with her, so He could not help her. Therefore, she chose to punish herself by not eating. She lived in this ongoing dual tension:

- Self-atonement: a desire to punish herself through fasting to soothe her guilty conscience.
- Self-centeredness: a desire for love that she could attain through her grades, even if it meant cheating.

Biffina's idolatrous craving for excellence, as defined by her dad, led her into an isolated, individualistic, and competitive way of thinking and behaving. The irony was that Biffina would bring her report card home to rave reviews at the end of each semester, the applause she longed to receive. Grandpa was happy. Grandma was happy. Daddy was happy. Mom was happy. Biffina was temporarily happy with their approval rating, but the gnawing away of her soul was an inconsolable burden that led to uncharacteristic acting-out behavior.

Sadly, her daddy was applauding her excellence while perplexed by her weight loss, oblivious to the acute longings of her soul and aiding her in the ongoing ensnaring to idolatry. Mable knew there was more to the issues but ignored the problems with Biff, hoping the counselor could correct everything. Biffina had all the answers but was not connecting the dots. The counselor collected the data and connected the dots, but now the family must determine if they want to address all the pertinent issues to help their daughter. Of course, that process would begin with Biff's recognition of his improper leadership and active repentance.

Call to Action

Describe how Biffina's unguarded strength had captured her soul. How were Biff and Mable complicit in Biffina's struggle? What were some of the dots they were not connecting, and what would you teach them to help them understand all the problems?

1. What are some of the things Biff must do to practicalize active repentance toward God and his family?
2. What would boasting in weakness mean to Biffina? How could Biff help her to implement this essential truth into her life?
3. In what specific ways does Mable need to repent to God, Biff, and Biffina?
4. What would you teach Biffina about God, and how would you work to make it stick? What would her repentance look like, practically speaking?

4

Standard Lowering

If our aim is perfection, we have two options. We can strive to be perfect through our strengths or accept someone else's perfection as ours. The first option is not tenable because we cannot live mistake-free unless we lower the high standard of perfection to meet its requirements, leaving us with the second option as a breath of fresh air. To have someone vouch for us by providing their perfection is grace unmerited and the privilege of every Christian.

Futile Perfection

Since none of us will ever be perfect, the most obvious solution is to find someone willing to give us their perfect standing. His name is Jesus, who gives us His alien righteousness. He was, is, and will always be the perfect Son of God. He cannot be otherwise; we cannot be anything but imperfect in our fallen condition. Some may ask, "Why would I not accept the gift of perfection from Jesus? What is it about me that compels me to reject His perfection while choosing to create an illusional world of perfection?" It's a valid question, so let me give you an illustration of someone who preferred the illusion over the perfection of Christ.

Biff had a hard time receiving criticism. Something in him recoiled every time someone expressed displeasure with him. To compensate, Biff strived hard for perfection, hoping he would avoid critique. The problem was that he could not hit his self-imposed perfect goal. Biff could not obey every Bible law, principle, assertion, implication, and expectation. Though unaware of the deception, his solution was to lower the Bible's standard. It was an unwitting cheapening of God's law so he could be perfect, which put him in a favorable light with others. Biff stacked the deck unbiblically, creating collateral damage, all because he wanted to look good in front of his peers. Let's look at what he did to lower God's law while elevating himself. Afterward, we'll assess the collateral damages.

LYING: Biff would lie to get himself out of a jam. Rather than owning the truth, he would twist it however much he needed to so he did not appear wrong before others. Biff would quickly tell you that he does not tell bald-faced lies. Correct. But Biff was lying just enough to skirt the truth. A little lie was not like big lies, a rationalization that soothed his conscience. He merely added to the truth or took away from the truth just enough to alter reality to suit his agenda. He had become so used to small deceptions that he did not recognize what he was doing to his conscience.

HARD CONSCIENCE: Through the subtle deceitfulness of sin, Biff's inner voice adjusted to accommodate his lying. His conscience was a means of grace to let him know when he was doing wrong (Romans 2:14–15). It's like a sound that goes off when we think about sinning. If we choose not to listen, our conscience will ring louder. Biff's conscience used to warn him when he was doing wrong. He chose to silence it through rationalizations. In time, his internal moral ringer consented, muting its sound (1 Timothy 4:2). Today, his conscience can hardly hear the bell (Hebrews 3:7, 4:7). It's like putting a piece of tape over the warning light on your dashboard—out of sight, out of mind. Biff's lies created a new normal, like a callus on the skin. Biff's heart lost sensitivity to where he could no longer discern right from wrong.

SELF-DECEPTION: As a tiny bird in a nest with its eyelids canvassed over, Biff had pulled the callused skin of subtle deception over his eyes. Biff had successfully cheapened the law to the point where he believed he was better than he was (Hebrews 5:12–14). Biff could not see what he could not see. He was not as stubborn as much as he was self-deceived. Biff could now pretend he was a successful perfectionist. On those rare moments where he knew that he had made a mistake, he justified, rationalized, or blamed the problem away. You can succeed as a perfectionist by exchanging the truth of God's Word. The problem with Biff was that his idolatrous desire to be perfect and his lying to cover up his imperfections blew up his marriage.

Collateral Damage

Mable, Biff's wife, was not as impressed with Biff. She saw through him and quickly let him know he was a fake. The perfect character he presented to her when they were dating was more like a Hollywood movie set—a facade. Once you walked through the door and entered his real life, there was no substance. Mable was never a person to mince words. She often reminded him of his failures. Telling a perfectionist that he is a fake is begging for trouble. I'm not suggesting that Biff's sin was Mable's, but she was guilty of not seeking to restore him in a spirit of gentleness (Galatians 6:1–3). Mable was emptying Biff's love cup, the metaphorical chalice he held out, expecting her to fill with the wine of affirmation, acceptance, and approval.

Mable had no inhibition from taking his love chalice and hitting him over the head with it. Rather than seeing the light, Biff began pulling away from his wife, initially entangling his mind in lustful thoughts. Because he could not satisfy the eye with seeing or fill the ear with hearing, wayward thoughts could not keep up with the idolatrous requirements (Ecclesiastes 1:8). Throw in the consistent reminders of failure from Mable. It did not take Biff long to see he needed another option to fill his cup. Biff had noticed an attractive lady who taught their son piano at their church. He began to look forward to each Sunday when he could drop his child off at the auditorium.

In time, he struck up a conversation with her. In time, they were involved in an adulterous affair. Biff knew it was wrong, but he did what he always has done—he justified his actions by blaming Mable. The idolatry of his heart overcame common sense and the grace of God. Eventually, they were found out, as those things typically go. Biff and Mable went to see their pastor for help. Biff wanted his marriage fixed, but he did not realize the insidious realities of his heart. The depth of his sin had so entangled him that Biff could not repent. He did not know what to repent from or how to make things right. Lack of awareness is a significant obstacle when helping a person like Biff.

Cheap Law

> Brothers, if anyone is caught in any transgression, you who are spiritual should restore him in a spirit of gentleness. Keep watch on yourself, lest you too be tempted.
> (Galatians 6:1)

> And we urge you, brothers, admonish the idle, encourage the fainthearted, help the weak, be patient with them all.
> (1 Thessalonians 5:14)

Biff has never had a clear view of himself, so what you think would be easy to discern and fix was a mystery to him. This problem is where God calls us to be careful how we talk to Biff and walk him through his sin. Biff's pastor had to skillfully navigate how to tell an insecure person, who strives for perfection, that he is not perfect. How do you tell someone who craves your approval that they are a failure? How do you tell a person who idolizes acceptance that he is unacceptable? Biff had lowered the law of God so low that he could obtain perfection.

> You therefore must be perfect, as your heavenly Father is perfect.
> (Matthew 5:48)

God requires Biff to be perfect, and Biff needs to be perfect. Mercifully, God provides a way for him to be perfect, but Biff rejects God's way as he strives for perfection his way. Biff does this by lowering the standard, altering his conscience, pretending to be okay, and justifying his actions when he does make a mistake. Biff's pastor had to elevate the law, convince him he was a failure, and appeal to him to trust the perfect Lamb of God. The first thing the pastor had to do was build a relational bridge with Biff. He had to become his friend. The pastor did not know Biff because of the size of their church, but he knew that he needed to build a bridge because the truth he had to carry to Biff could push him further into his idolatry.

No Gradations

Biff did not make it easy for his pastor. He was quick to tell him about his high-powered job and philanthropic endeavors. Biff was boasting in his strengths. He was elevating himself in front of his pastor. Do you see why Biff could not see what he was doing to himself? Do you see how difficult it was for his pastor to readjust Biff's thinking to a more precise and biblical reality? After a few sessions, the pastor did recalibrate Biff. Eventually, the pastor began to roll out the gospel in a way that Biff had never heard before. He only understood the gospel through the lens of salvation.

Biff had no clue how to bring the gospel to bear on his sanctification. Biff believed God saved him by grace (Ephesians 2:8–9), but he also thought he had to be perfect post-salvation. Biff was willing to accept that he was a lowdown sinner who needed a Savior, but it wasn't as noticeable how to live a progressively sanctified life. Biff began to learn that he would never be able to create a righteousness that God would accept. Biff would never be acceptable to God based on his works, whether those works were pre- or post-salvation. On his best day, he was a beggar needing God's grace (1 Timothy 1:15).

There was only one rung on the ladder that Biff earned, the lowest. There are no other levels of righteousness in God's world. All people are bottom-rung sinners, Christ is the perfectly righteous top-rung Savior, and there is no in-between. We stay on the bottom rung or accept Christ's alien righteousness and live in His perfection. When this truth clicked inside Biff's head, he expelled air from his lungs. It was like he could breathe again. The chains of perfectionism had bound him into a pleasing others, craving approval worldview. He never realized the depth of his bondage. Then it clicked.

Being, Not Doing

Biff learned that it was not about doing things but about being something. He had never experienced shalom in Jesus. He was never at peace because he always felt he had to work for acceptance. Embracing nothing and being nobody was a foreign concept. Biff began to understand, and the more this gospel penetrated his mind, the more he experienced release from selfish ambition and reputation management. This new gospel orientation encouraged him to serve his wife rather than manipulate her to fill his love cup. Rather than being a man with demands for love—the way he wanted it, he became a man with a servant's heart.

He became like Christ, the perfect example of others-centered living (Mark 10:45). Biff did not have to cheapen the law or lower it to achieve his standard of perfection. He elevated the law, as lived out through Christ. Oddly, the more he raised the law, the more joy he experienced. After he realized that he could not keep God's moral standard, he started praising God for the Son who did obey what the law demanded. Rather than trying to impress others, he became more impressed with Jesus. The more impressed he became with the Son, the more he was inclined to imitate the Son. The more he was inclined to imitate the Son, the more he impacted those around him, especially his wife.

But it became even odder for Biff and Mable. The more he grew in Christlikeness through his humble servanthood, the more she loved him in return. Ironically, Biff got the very thing he desired—the love and acceptance of his wife, but it did not come because he demanded it, deserved it, or faked perfection. She loves him because Biff loves God with all his heart, soul, mind, and strength (Luke 10:27). He loves God so much because he knows he is a low-down, dirty, rotten sinner who recognizes that he deserves hell, but Christ came to give him a perfection he could never attain through his effort, creating a gravitational pull that his wife could not resist.

Call to Action

1. In what way have you lowered the Word of God to make yourself look better before others?
2. When we do this, we exchange the truth of God for a lie, worshipping the creature more than the Creator. What does this thought mean to you?
3. Why do people create edited versions of themselves for public consumption? What are some mechanisms to perpetuate these lies, i.e., justification and rationalization? How does this mindset affect the soul, i.e., the conscience?
4. If you were counseling Biff and Mable, what would you like to know from them, and what would you like to tell them?
5. What will you say to Mable to help her repent? She did not like Biff when he did not meet her expectations, but she likes him now. What if Biff fails again? What does Mable need to do to guard her heart against future temptation?

5

Perfect Problems

Striving for self-generated perfection is as futile as attempting to save ourselves because it perpetuates internal turmoil and frustrates our closest friends. Though God does not want us to live sloppy, haphazard lives, He does want us to know that perfection comes through our weaknesses—our inability to be perfect, not our strengths. The appeal of God's Word is clear; if we boast, make it in our weaknesses, accompanied by His miraculous strength that operates in us.

The Trifecta

Biff is a perfectionist. At least, that is the persona he presents. It is maddening to Mable, his wife. Biff says absolute excellence in all things is how you glorify God. He is particular about how to do things and explicitly explains why his way is better and more pleasing to God. Mable tried to help him see how striving for perfection is detrimental to his relationship with God and her, but Biff is not your average Christian. He is relentless in his pursuit of excellence. There is something profound inside that drives him to perfection. If you were to counsel Mable to come alongside Biff as a gentle restorer (Galatians 6:1-3), what are a few things you'd like for her to know? How would you guide her?

I will assume two of those things would be his

presupposition and worldview. A presupposition is what he thinks before he thinks, his pre-thoughts that give meaning to his thoughts. His presupposition forms the window through which all his thoughts find an interpretation. E.g., if his window is blue, he interprets life through a blue lens. His worldview is the substance of those interpretations. His presupposition creates his worldview. His worldview motivates him to strive for perfection.

Three primary shaping influences in Biff's life have created his presuppositional, interpretive filter. The first one is Adam. After Adam became imperfect through the fall, he tried to compensate by becoming perfect. Biff inherited Adam's presupposition—for all have sinned (Romans 3:23, 5:12). The second negative shaping influence was Biff's dad. He was managed and manipulated by a heavy-handed, non-encouraging, authoritarian father. Talking to Biff years later, he tears up as he shares how impossible it was to please his dad. God saved him as an adult, but he landed in a legalistic religious church culture where following the rules was paramount. It was the trifecta: Adam, early adverse childhood influences, and Christian legalism.

Parading Perfectionist

Born in Adam officially stamps us as legalists. Adam wanted his works to matter, and so do we. Christianity is the only religion in the world where our works cannot save us. Unfortunately, that little truth does not keep individuals from smuggling their performances onto their resumes to impress others. You can take the boy out of Adam and put him in Christ, but you cannot take Adam out of the boy—not until the boy gets a glorified body. When you put the boy, whose daddy manipulated him to strive for acceptance as a child, in a larger group of like-minded legalists, guess what? You are going to have a legalistic religious culture.

The legalism that drives perfectionism is an illusionary

lifestyle. It only works if we can hide our real problems—our true selves—by avoiding public scrutiny. Think fig leaves (Genesis 3:7). If we can keep our issues hidden, we can present ourselves well in a performance-based religious culture that pursues righteousness and harshly judges mistakes. The temptations to self-deception and perpetuating deception in these cultures are strong. Parading as a perfectionist is high-end, religious game-playing that needs the disinfecting light of the gospel.

The game is that if your trouble does not transcend your ability to present yourself well, you can live in a legalistic culture. What happens too often is that relational conflict and personal problems steadily increase until we cannot keep the pretense going any longer. Biff is nearing the breaking point. He needs a courageous, competent, and compassionate friend who can help him to see what he cannot see. The desire to please others is classic fear of man (Proverbs 29:25). Perfectionists always try to please someone.

- They are trying to please God.
- They are trying to please others.
- They are trying to please themselves.

Biblical Thinking

This last point—pleasing yourself—speaks to the man who has a human-centered view of what excellence should be and is striving to hit this self-imposed standard to self-approve or self-congratulate himself. While the first two scenarios require other people to be his audience—God or people—this last deception differs because he lives in a self-contained universe where the performer and the audience are the same. Regardless of who he is seeking approval from, something rooted in his heart motivates him to strive for aspirations only the LORD can provide.

Perfectionism is a twisted and dangerous theology, though it is not the best word to describe what is going on with Biff. However, that word can serve as a portal to a more biblical typology. Perfectionism is a cultural concept that can start the conversation, but it is always better to push for theological precision. The closer you get to the Bible's way of talking about our problems, the better you can identify what is going on in the perfectionist's heart and bring biblically precise care to the person. A better definition will permit you to do these four things:

- Know what to look for in the person you want to help.
- Sort out what applies and does not apply to him.
- Discern what you have through an assessment and elimination process.
- Bring biblical solutions based on a biblically filtered person.

Here are eight things I would look for if I were counseling Biff. I'm not saying they all are valid for him, but I would want to run him through a biblical filter to have a clearer picture of the person I'm trying to help.

1. **PARTIAL OBEDIENCE:** You can only be perfect in what you are good at. Selective perfection is where God's theology and Biff's theology collide. The LORD says Biff is not perfect and will never be perfect outside of Christ, so to over-strive for perfection is at odds with who God says he is and how he achieves biblical perfection. On his best day, he will fail. While giving all his life and projects his best shot is nice, Biff must be a biblical realist. He cannot hit perfection in every area of his life. A person motivated toward unbiblical and unrealistic excellence will be dysfunctional in other vital

areas of his life. He will spend most of his time performing in ways that guarantee success because he will always work within his strengths.

2. **INTELLECTUAL DISHONESTY:** You will find inconsistencies in Biff's life. It will not be hard to discover them because a few threads will hang out of his garments whenever he tries to be something he is not. There will be areas where he is failing, and you hope he will be honest about those imperfections. To try to sell perfectionism as a way of life is not honest. Their commitment to his excellent worldview will reveal the level of dishonesty and deception at work. While you can give him a hall pass for ignorance, you will find more than blindness in his life. There will be deception and deceit that may have twisted his thinking. "Claiming to be wise, they became fools" (Romans 1:22).

3. **UNCONFESSED SINS:** Do not be surprised to find unadmitted sinfulness. Everybody knows they are finite, a reality that implies limitations or God-imposed boundaries (Genesis 11:1–9) that keep individuals from ascending too high in their estimation of themselves. The perfectionist has lost touch with biblical reality, and if he persists in this kind of thinking, he will have to alter his perceptions about himself, God, and life. He must twist the truth to grind out his pursuit of excellence. This process is futile thinking (Romans 1:21; Ephesians 4:17–19). A typical way this works out is to make excuses for the things he cannot do well. If he strives for perfection—an unattainable goal at best—he must explain why he fails in areas where he cannot meet his perfectionistic standard.

4. **RELATIONAL FALLOUT:** The perfectionist will be self-justifying, rationalizing, and excuse-making,

creating relational tension. Ask Mable. One of the tricks in the bag of the perfectionist is to put others down through critique, condemnation, and regular reminders of where they have missed the mark. Putting others down has a self-elevating effect: "If I put you down, I am maintaining a higher standard than you. If I cannot be perfect, I must be deceptive by being a self-righteous critique-er of others." The fallout from this will be horrible. The perfectionist lives in a world where he acts superior while his wife, children, and friends look on with saddened faces as they watch the emperor with no clothes.

5. **Missed Opportunities:** The people who will be hurt the most are his wife and children. All high-demand, excellent-driven spouses or parents will decimate their families. Trying to execute perfection in children has horrifying effects. Children are imperfect on their best days. They are sobering pictures of who we all are before God the Father. Rather than pushing people to perfection, Christ came alongside individuals to let them know they could never be perfect. Rather than making them be what they could never be, He gave them what they needed. He shepherded them to the cross, inviting them to pursue His perfection. There are redemptive purposes found in the gospel, and what better place to bring care to others than through their imperfections? The perfectionist does not perceive these redemptive opportunities. Demanding, critiquing, and being harsh or unkind reveals a total misunderstanding of the doctrine of sin and how the gospel connects to our imperfections.

6. **Fighting God:** Ultimately, this is a spiritual battle for Biff. He is in a battle of wills with the LORD. I am talking about pride here, the one thing God will

resist in any human (James 4:6). The LORD did not come for perfect people. He came for the sick, the wounded, the needy, the incomplete, the weak, and the imperfect. The perfectionist attempts to put on perfection outside of God's grace. These were the Pharisees during the time of Christ. They saw perfection as the chief end of man and had no problem sporting perfection on their shirt sleeves (Matthew 23:5).

7. **COMPETING STRENGTHS:** There is an argument to be made by the perfectionist that excellence is a great way to glorify God. There is some truth here, but it is only a partial truth. People should always strive to be better and do better. The solutions are not to seek perfection because you are a perfectionist or to give up as though sloppiness is the only way to accrue God's favor. There is another way to glorify God. The gospel is our chief witness for how humanity could make a mess of things, yet what Christ did was the most life-altering, world-shaking thing a man has ever done. The person who refuses to understand how God makes His strength perfect in human imperfection will always be weak, even though he has twisted his mind to think he's strong (2 Corinthians 12:10). Jesus died on a tree. Christ's friends were looking for something, shall I say, a bit more perfect than a man dying on a tree. They could not, at least not then, wrap their minds around how the foolishness and weakness of God could be wiser and stronger than them (1 Corinthians 1:18–25). Biff can either exalt his or Christ's strength, but he cannot do both. (See 2 Corinthians 1:8–9, 4:7, and 12:7–10.) If he chooses to compete with God, he will lose.

8. **GOSPEL DISCONNECT:** To think that humanly derived, perfect processes lead to perfect outcomes

flies in the face of the gospel. From a man-centered worldview, this makes sense because there is logic there. But God defies logic, which is one way He shows us how the foolishness and weakness of God can thwart our world's wisdom. We must believe that the LORD's strength will work through us. Biff needs to see these things. He needs to be honest. Biff needs to find rest in Christ. He needs contentment. Biff has yet to learn the secret of life: "For when I am weak, then I am strong" (2 Corinthians 12:10). Paul also said,

I have learned in whatever situation I am to be content. I know how to be brought low, and I know how to abound. In any and every circumstance, I have learned the secret of facing plenty and hunger, abundance and need. I can do all things through him who strengthens me.
(Philippians 4:11–13)

Call to Action

1. How have the three primary shaping influences in Biff's life—Adam, authorities, and religion—molded him?
2. Considering these three influences, how would you counsel Biff regarding each one?
3. What would your counsel be to Mable to guide Biff through his former manner of life?
4. What about the gospel that has yet to connect with Biff, and how will you share it with him?
5. What is Biff afraid of, why is he that way, and what is a practical path forward as you care for him?
6. Develop a practical counseling plan to help him mature. Create eight sequential mile markers to move him along and fill in the framework of each session.

6

Perfect Praise

Utopia does not exist on planet Earth. It's a mirage in a desert. It's like someone attempting to be perfect; he does not exist, either. My goal here is not to rain on anyone's parade but to help gain a better perspective on living well in God's world while releasing ourselves from pursuing the unrealistic, nonexistent perfect life. My concern is that some of us are uncomfortable in our skin, and as we stare at our imperfections, we hope to find something more perfect. If you're that striving soul, I have excellent news for you; God's strength needs your imperfection to magnify His fame for your good.

Imperfect Signs

I trust you always strive to improve, be better, and live well in God's world. I'm not suggesting passivity, resignation, losing hope, or ceasing to do your part to love God and others well. The key to striving for your best life now is to do it with the correct information, which means we must factor imperfection into our plans. Everywhere we look, we see signs of imperfection.

- I will always have a lower intellectual ceiling than others.
- I struggle with aspects of becoming older.
- I will not experience sinless perfection in my mortal

body.
- On my best days, a little bit of hypocrisy resides in me.
- Some of my friends are not Christians and never shall be.
- Jesus died on the cross, a horrible event.
- Paul could not get rid of his thorn in the flesh.
- If I dropped a cone of ice cream on the floor, it would land upside down.

What Women Want

Consider a woman's fear of becoming older, less significant, or less attractive. The fear of aging is a big deal for some women, as they labor under the burden of our culture's propagated view of physicality and sexuality. The world's worldview tempts women to overthink sexuality and beauty. Their thoughts oscillate from overeating to under-eating, shopping, exercising, and physical alterations. You name it. If you examine their heart motivations closely, you will find some familiar foes: envy, jealousy, judging, bitterness, anger, discontentment, depression, shame, cynicism, fear, worry, and anxiety.

Though some women may appear to be free and empowered—the hope of feminists everywhere—they are, in reality, culturally enslaved people. Internal pressures bind their souls while transforming their bodies into objects that represent how they want others to perceive them. Whatever they believe is the expected way to be is the goal they seek to become. This kind of soul discontentment leaves them frustrated and fearful. They never capture the elusive beauty carrot, though they always crave it, while the beauty of Christ is a faint echo of Christian tradition (Psalm 27:4; 1 Peter 3:4). It is a horrible way for any Christian woman to live.

What Men Want

Many men are in lives we do not like because we tie our reputations to the culture's view of success. We want bigger and better, and just like a woman gazing over the beauty competition, we measure ourselves by our ability to look good in front of others. Coming up short or missing the mark is not an option for culturally enslaved men. This lie from the devil has been placed deep in our hearts. He was the one who first said God is not enough, and Adam and Eve submitted to his dastardly doctrine, and the rest of us fell in line with the deception (Genesis 3:1–7; Romans 5:12).

Nearly all counseling happens because somebody does not measure up; there is an undercurrent of dissatisfaction with something about themselves or a relationship that somehow connects to them. The counselee is unwilling (or they do not know how) to live imperfectly with imperfect people. I'm not suggesting they should not change, but the sweet spot of contentment is somewhere between striving for perfection and a lack of interest in changing.

No matter where we turn, people are frustrated. The only thing that will make them happy is if their circumstances change to get what they want. When not getting what we desire tempts us to sin, we have an idol in our lives. Though we must always work out what God is working into us, we do this with the peace of God ruling our hearts. Perhaps responding to the following statement would provide the best analysis a person needs to see who or what has rulership over their heart. Whatever you place in the blank, other than the Lord, is idolatry (Exodus 20:3). "I could be satisfied if _____."

Six Idolators

As you ponder this statement, will you reflect on these six people? Their struggles are common to all of us. See if you can see what has rulership over their hearts. Perhaps thinking through these few scenarios would help to capture the practical essence of how our hearts succumb to temptation so easily.

- A teenage girl senses discontentment by the gnawing fear that eats at her.
- A wife is frustrated because her husband is not a good protector or lover.
- A husband is angry because his wife has changed from the person he married.
- A friend is bothered because someone is a pain in their rear end.
- A church member is annoyed because the church is not doing a better job caring for folks.
- An employee is dissatisfied because he is not climbing the company ladder.

The things that manage us characterize our general attitude and disposition during any given day, bringing us to the all-important question: what controls you? Who or what has the most power over you? Does the Lord control your mind and emotions? What is the thing that tempts you to take your thoughts away from the stabilizing influence of the Lord? The most effective way to answer these questions is by how you respond when you do not get what you want. Let's return to our six friends. We would want to ask them some obvious questions if we had a relationship, opportunity, and context to care for them.

- What controls you?
- Where do you find your identity?

- What gives you your primary satisfaction?
- When you feel empty, how do you seek to be refilled?

Rethinking Imperfection

Did you know there is a counterintuitive way of thinking about imperfection? What if we turned our imperfection on its head? Rather than trying to solve the problem of imperfection by changing ourselves, our friends, or our circumstances, what if we saw our imperfections as a means of grace for the Lord to use in our lives? Could the Lord want imperfection in our lives for our good and His glory? We find a clear example of this in 2 Corinthians 12:7-10. Paul's temptation was to think too highly of himself. The Lord knew this, so He gave Paul a gift—a thorn in the flesh to harass His chosen servant.

> So to keep me from becoming conceited because of the surpassing greatness of the revelations, a thorn was given me in the flesh, a messenger of Satan to harass me, to keep me from becoming conceited.
> (2 Corinthians 12:7)

God gave this imperfection to help Paul become all he should be through Christ's strength rather than his own (Philippians 4:11-13). Sometimes the harassment you feel in your life is from your loving Lord. He is harassing you to help you rely on Him rather than yourself. He gives you an imperfect life for His glory and your good. Paul did not readily embrace his imperfect life. He figured he could do more without a thorn than with one. What about you? I am not saying you should resign to an imperfect life challenge, especially if the desired changes are biblical. What I am saying is your circumstances may not change, and if they do not, you have to guard your heart against responding sinfully to those unchanging conditions.

Reasons to Praise

Suppose you regularly sin because your life, associations, or situations are not changing according to your hopes and expectations. In that case, idolatry has captured you. Sinful responses do not force the hand of God. Sinful reactions attract the opposing power of God in your life. The Lord will not partner with you or your sin if your motives, attitudes, and actions are not godly (James 4:6). What if the Lord could use sin sinlessly in your life? You know, the way He did with Joseph (Genesis 50:20), with Paul (2 Corinthians 12:7-10), and the way He did with His Son (Isaiah 53:10). What if the Lord never wants to remove what you believe to be imperfect, wrong, or unfair? What if the Lord was the Author of your imperfection because He knows it is for your good (Romans 8:28)? I can think of at least four reasons He would do this for you.

1. **IMPERFECTION EXISTS:** I will not belabor this point because it is a fact: we will never attain perfection in this life. We are fallen individuals who live in a fallen world with other fallen people. There is an imperfect ceiling, and we live under it. The Lord has set the bounds (Genesis 11:6-7) of our lives just like any good and loving parent would set the limits to their child's life. It is one of the early and essential lessons for any child (Acts 17:26-27).

   Son, you are not omnipotent, omniscient, or omnipresent. You work within limits. God has made you a certain way, and the sooner you figure out what way that is and become copacetic with that way, the better off you will be.
   —Dad

2. **IMPERFECTION REMINDS:** Paul needed reminding that he was not God. The Lord had blessed him with many revelations, which became a temptation source. It was not suitable for him to live in a frictionless world. Like all our strengths, they can quickly become liabilities if we do not regularly humble ourselves before the Gift Giver. We are no different from Nebuchadnezzar, who lost sight of what he had, thinking the world revolved around him (Daniel 4:28–37).

3. **IMPERFECTION DRIVES:** If we understand our faults rightly, we will see them as vehicles to get to God rather than hindrances to a better life (2 Corinthians 1:8–9). Typically, the things perceived as wrong will move us in one of two directions. We will experience imperfection and turn to the Lord, or we will experience imperfection and turn to self-reliant means to resolve the imperfection. Our imperfections should humble us while driving us to the Lord. Since Genesis 3, humanity has possessed a two-option system: we turn toward God or move toward destructive choices.

4. **IMPERFECTION PERMITS:** The beauty of our imperfections is they permit us to find God and enjoy Him while finding strength through Him. This perspective is vital when thinking about the wrong things in our lives. It explains why Paul repented from his complaining while embracing his imperfection. He learned the secret to his best life now. It was not through perfection but imperfection (2 Corinthians 12:10).

Call to Action

> *I have learned in whatever situation I am to be content. I know how to be brought low, and I know how to abound. In any and every circumstance, I have learned the secret of facing plenty and hunger, abundance and need. I can do all things through him who strengthens me.*
> (Philippians 4:11–13)

The wise person can live in an imperfect world. This person is constantly striving toward Christ while understanding some of the means to enjoy Christ may come through personal weakness and disappointment (Matthew 16:24; Philippians 1:29). The wise person does not give up on pursuing excellence but the things that are not his at this moment do not control him. The wise person has learned the wisdom of Paul. Think about the next major decision you want to make. Maybe it's not a big decision, but you must decide so you can move forward.

1. How does your striving for comfort or control impact your decision-making?
2. How does your fear of not getting what you desire influence the decision you need to make?
3. Now that you know there are no perfect choices, can you rest rather than fret about what you must do?
4. When you make your "pro and con list," consider how the Lord's fame could spread by not getting what you want?

7

Need to Die

Dying to ourselves is the hardest thing we will ever do, and it's not a one-time appointment with God. Death to self is a repeated act of submitting ourselves to the Lord. The good news is that He helps us in this life-long process by incrementally, systematically, and purposely putting us to death. Did you know God is working behind the scenes to undermine our remaining self-reliance so we can trust Him more effectively? Sometimes He must sabotage our self-sufficiency to teach us to rely on Him who raises the dead.

Exhibit A

> For we were so utterly burdened beyond our strength that we despaired of life itself. Indeed, we felt that we had received the sentence of death. But that was to make us rely not on ourselves but on God.
> (2 Corinthians 1:8–9a)

Exhibit A for this kind of teaching is the apostle Paul. He had a God-ordained difficult life. He endured many hardships. Why? Because he knew Christ. A relationship with Christ prevents us from foregoing suffering (Luke 14:26–27). It's the opposite! Knowing Christ ensures suffering. To know Jesus is a call to die (Luke 9:23). For Paul, suffering was not a lifestyle to spurn but a means God used to push him to true greatness. Paul's understanding of the mysteries of suffering gives us several serious questions to ponder.

- For example, what animates your innermost thoughts?
- What drives your greatest desires?
- Is it your amazement at knowing Christ and being known by Him, or is it a desire for a better life than you currently have?

Knowing Christ and being able to tell others about Christ was the purpose of Paul's life. This singular animating passion did not coexist with a need to overcome his problems. He knew better. He perceived the point of his problems—to enable him to put Christ on display more effectively. Suffering in Paul's life was like a magnifying glass. It allowed him to magnify Christ to his sphere of influence (Psalm 34:3). Suffering is one of those mysteries God gives us so that we can understand Him more deeply. Equipped with Paul's theology of suffering, we can enjoy a more profound life with the Lord. It is a maturity that does not make suffering disappear. It is the suffering that fuels and sustains Christlike maturity.

> That I may know him and the power of his resurrection, and may share his sufferings, becoming like him in his death.
> (Philippians 3:10)

> I have been crucified with Christ. It is no longer I who live, but Christ who lives in me. And the life I now live in the flesh I live by faith in the Son of God, who loved me and gave himself for me.
> (Galatians 2:20)

> Truly, truly, I say to you, unless a grain of wheat falls into the earth and dies, it remains alone; but if it dies, it bears much fruit.
>
> (John 12:24)

Celebrate Recovery

One of the unintended consequences of the biblical counseling movement is that some people believe counseling is a means to make their problems disappear. Some counselors succumb to this expectation, creating pressure on themselves to help counselees resolve their problems according to how they want resolution. Imagine if the great apostle Paul came to you with a thorn in his flesh. Imagine you knew he was a profoundly spiritual man who loved God wholeheartedly and was doggedly determined to tell others about Christ. He was a mature Christian, not a nominal one.

Furthermore, he told you about his problem and how he had committed it to prayer, asking God to remove his thorn. He has come to you because he wants your help eliminating the harassing intruder. Here is crucial information: God is not, will not, cannot, and should not remove this thorn from Paul's life. Paul will live the rest of his life with his thorn. It is God's irrevocable will for your counselee, Paul. What if you believed it was your job to help Paul get rid of his problem according to how Paul perceived it? In the culture, it's called affirmative care, where the counselee determines the outcome. God did not write the Bible so that we can celebrate recovery. Paul never recovered that way.

> Three times I pleaded with the Lord about this, that it should leave me. But he said to me, "My grace is sufficient for you, for my power is made perfect in weakness."
>
> (2 Corinthians 12:8–9a)

But he is unchangeable, and who can turn him back? What he desires, that he does. For he will complete what he appoints for me, and many such things are in his mind.

(Job 23:13–14)

Gospel Transformation

The celebration we see in the Scriptures is a Savior who transforms us through the power of the gospel, which sometimes happens by not removing the thorns in our lives. He did not come to give us a great marriage, a disease-free body, and financial freedom. Though there are present, earthly benefits to living godly while humbly applying the truths of the Word of God to our lives, the problem-free priorities and expectations that most people in our culture consider a right are not promises. Our culture is trying to figure out how to overcome their disappointments through human-centered therapies.

The God-centered Christian has found a better way by celebrating the transformation that shapes a person into the likeness of Jesus Christ. So often, this kind of change happens because of the suffering in our lives. The biblical realist knows he cannot escape all sorrow. The realist also knows that suffering and the good life are not always hostile to each other. Disciplers, pastors, and counselors must be clear on this matter. They must not make problem removal their number one goal for two reasons. It could be that God wants them to keep their thorn stuck in their flesh because that is the best way for the person to put His Son on display. It could be that God wants them to get rid of their thorn in the flesh because that is the best way for the individual to put His Son on display.

Our primary goal should be to put Jesus on display in our lives regardless of how God chooses to accomplish it. This worldview leads to an all-important question: how do you want to define your life? Are you more interested in displaying God's name through your suffering? Are you more interested in removing your suffering, regardless if it brings glory to God? The therapeutic culture promises to get rid of their problems. God promises to find strength through our problems.

To Suffer or Not

> Therefore I will boast all the more gladly of my weaknesses, so that the power of Christ may rest upon me. For the sake of Christ, then, I am content with weaknesses, insults, hardships, persecutions, and calamities. For when I am weak, then I am strong.
>
> (2 Corinthians 12:9b-10)

> For to this you have been called, because Christ also suffered for you, leaving you an example, so that you might follow in his steps.
>
> (1 Peter 2:21)

Jesus came to die on the cross so that we could have an example to follow. We must walk in His steps to find a better life. When sin came into the world, violence, disease, and corruption came along for the ride. Every person became a bad person (Isaiah 64:6; Romans 3:10-12), and bad things happen to bad people. Christ did not come to die to change violence, disease, or corruption. He came to change lives. Though the death and resurrection of the Savior have slowed down the onslaught of sin, it was not the point of the gospel. His point was to give us His life so we could be in Him while looking forward to a better world (Hebrews 11:10).

We find our strength, glory, hope, and praise in God rather than in a perfect relationship or a healthy body. It's a person's unwillingness to embrace this kind of theology of suffering that opens the door to discouragement and depression. The longer it takes a person to find strength in suffering, the more susceptible they will be to discouragement. Our therapeutic culture opposes this teaching because they are beholden to an anti-suffering, utopian message. Part of the American dream is to remove all suffering from everyone, which is untenable teaching that does not factor in the doctrine of fallenness.

If you want to rid yourself of your problems but cannot get to that utopian place, you will experience disappointment. If medications do not work or if a divorce does not give you a better life, you will not be far from depression. How influenced have you become by our culture's best life now mantra? How has the prosperity drumbeat detracted you from the Christological purposes of your life? You can measure how you think about these questions by examining how you respond to the complex challenges in your life. If you have peace, hope, and rest amid your deepest trials, the culture's suffering-free promise has not arrested and entrapped you.

In Search of Weakness

If you're going to walk with God, it is not your strength that God will use. He can't. He won't. He will not compete with you. He puts His treasure in clay jars (2 Corinthians 4:7). God works through weakness and brokenness, not personal might or high intellect (Zechariah 4:6). Your weakness will release His strength that He perfects in you. If your primary purpose in life is to be healthy and wealthy, you will be working counter to the purposes of God, and your frustrations will mount. Resisting God's suffering-centric plans for you will send you into a black hole of hopelessness. The way up is most assuredly down. The gospel narrative always cuts against the grain of the world's narrative (1 Corinthians 1:25).

The counterintuitive gospel does not mean being sick, poor, and having dysfunctional relationships are God's only ways to provide His strength. The idea here is not celebrating sin or suffering but celebrating Christ regardless of our circumstances. We can only be strong by living in God's strength, not our own. We can only overcome this by celebrating God's strength through our weakness, brokenness, sickness, and poverty. Let me reiterate: I am not saying you should contract HIV to be strong. I'm not saying you should intentionally become bankrupt to unleash God's power in your life. I'm saying that our circumstances, whatever they are, become a means to find God's strength, hope, peace, and contentment.

It could be that God will choose to raise you from unfavorable circumstances, but that cannot be your first or most important prayer request. Your first and greatest desire must be to die in Christ, unleashing God's perfected power in your life (John 12:24). Prayer is the beginning of embracing Christ's death as your soul-sustaining strength. Ask the Father to help you walk through Christ's incremental, systematic, and purposeful death (Galatians 2:20). The Lord will help you die to yourself (Isaiah 53:10). You must let go of your strength to hold on to His strength. Perhaps this sample prayer from the Valley of Vision prayer book may guide you in grasping some of these more profound truths.

Valley of Vision

> Lord, high and holy, meek and lowly, Thou hast brought me to the valley of vision, where I live in the depths but see Thee in the heights; hemmed in by mountains of sin I behold Thy glory.
>
> Let me learn by paradox that the way down is the way up, that to be low is to be high, that the broken heart is the healed heart, that the contrite spirit is

the rejoicing spirit, that the repenting soul is the victorious soul, that to have nothing is to possess all, that to bear the cross is to wear the crown, that to give is to receive, that the valley is the place of vision.

Lord, in the daytime stars can be seen from deepest wells, and the deeper the wells the brighter Thy stars shine; let me find Thy light in my darkness, Thy life in my death, Thy joy in my sorrow, Thy grace in my sin, Thy riches in my poverty, Thy glory in my valley.

Call to Action

1. Will you discuss your theology of suffering with a friend? What does that term mean to you, practically speaking?
2. Perhaps spending a season praying this Valley of Vision prayer would serve your soul well.
3. Are you struggling? What do you believe God's good intentions are for you as you struggle?
4. Are you finding God's strength in your weakness? Perhaps this would be an excellent time to talk to someone about this. If your weakness is not manifesting God's strength, what might be the problem? Will you share your thoughts with a friend?
5. Is there something you want more than Christ as your animating center? I am not saying you have to lose what you want, but are you willing to lose it if it is the only way to find peace and strength with God (Luke 22:42)?

8

Beyond Your Ability

Did you know God puts you in spots where He expects you to fail? This perspective might sound harsher than it is at first glance. But what if God could use your sins, mistakes, shortcomings, and weaknesses for your good and His glory? Have you ever considered how your disappointments and discouragements could provide the backdrop for the Lord to demonstrate His power and goodness through your inabilities and missteps? It's true. God's strength coming through our weakness is one of the many ways He proves His love to us.

Not Supposed to Succeed

> But we have this treasure in jars of clay, to show that the surpassing power belongs to God and not to us.
> (2 Corinthians 4:7)

My friend Mable used to be part of the disappointed and discouraged crowd. She was an overworked, over-challenged, and overwhelmed single mom. She lived in a world where she never seemed to get on top of things. Initially, her tenacious grit compelled her to try harder. She bought into the culture's worldview of independence and self-reliance. She determined never to lose and never give up. It was a win-win at all costs, and no matter how difficult things became, her mantra was, "When things get tough, the tough get going." Her perspective worked well until her meltdowns outnumbered her victories. Finally, her boss called her in and gave her an ultimatum—no more outbursts. She freaked.

Rather than seeking God, she gave herself over to fear and worry, which eventually turned into bitterness and compounded anxiety. Then the depression came calling. Mable's internal turmoil put her between a rock and a hard place—to the point where she thought about suicide. She considered counseling in a last-ditch effort to pull herself out of her funk. After listening to her story of woe for nearly an hour, I said, "God is calling you to do what you cannot do with the ability you do not have." She gave me a quizzical look, which I followed with, "He wants it this way. What you're going through is the will of God for your life. God wants to bring you to a place where you cannot fix yourself or your life because His desire is for you to rely on Him."

> For we do not want you to be unaware, brothers, of the affliction we experienced in Asia. For we were so utterly burdened beyond our strength that we despaired of life itself. Indeed, we felt that we had received the sentence of death. But that was to make us rely not on ourselves but on God who raises the dead.
>
> (2 Corinthians 1:8–9)

Your Attention, Please

A suffering-sending God was mysteriously complex for her to hear initially. She was embarrassed about not being able to do it all by herself. Everything that could go wrong was going wrong, and no matter how hard Mable tried to keep it all together, it was unraveling even faster. Her response was to internalize her problems, never utter a word, and redouble her efforts, but her plan was not working. She could not keep up anymore. She was done.

- She had no husband.
- All her friends were stay-at-home moms.
- Her kids wore hand-me-downs.
- She could not afford family vacations.
- Her car was a clunker.
- She had to pull the children out of private school.
- Her ex-husband was an every-other-weekend unholy terror.

Sometimes life is meant to go wrong because it is the only way God can get our attention. He had Mable's attention now. She was crying out for help. A plea for help, out of a heart of genuine brokenness, is the prayer He was leading her to repeat back to Him. Mable had to come to the place where we all should come. She said the quiet part aloud: "I am not self-reliant." God never intended for us to win all the time. Sometimes God has to run us into a ditch to free us from ourselves. The self-sufficient person does not need God. It is a deceptive and tempting approach to life that does not work. Paul was right: "I can do all things through him who strengthens me," not through me who strengthens me (Philippians 4:13).

The Win-win Disorder

To say, "I can do all things through me who strengthens me," is a worship disorder of the worst kind. It is not God's intention to let us do things our way, according to our agenda, while working within our personal gifting and well-honed skillset (Genesis 11:6). It can never be win-win all the time for all people, with or without God. He is too merciful to allow this to happen to His fallen creation. He insists we do things according to His will while He receives glory for what He accomplishes through us (Romans 11:36; Philippians 2:12-13). The implication is clear: there will be times when God will accomplish things outside our abilities.

We need to understand this. We are to work under His power and strength rather than our own. Part of this is because people are "glory hogs." Isn't it true that we love praise and adoration? We desire to be like a god (Genesis 3:5), which is at the heart of our self-reliant, Adamic fallenness problem. This kind of self-centered thinking puts us in competition with God, as well as with others. We demand our way; God requires His way. Guess who is going to win that tug-of-war? To help us get over ourselves, the Lord mercifully puts us in places or situations where we cannot control or manipulate the outcomes, which happened to Mable.

She had two choices. She could stubbornly press on to her shame and other people's hurt, or she could relinquish her rights to her situation and trust God's way—even if it did not make sense. Here are a few examples of times when God's way is challenging to embrace. Will you read over these questions and honestly analyze yourself? Which is easier, to respond in your strength or God's strength?

- When it's time to forgive someone who has hurt you.
- When it's time to regularly submit to and serve your spouse (Ephesians 5:21).
- When it's time to ask forgiveness first.
- When it is time to share your inner struggles with your friends.
- When it's time to seek forgiveness from someone you believe has a worse sin than yours.

Beyond Our Ability

Did you know God is regularly testing us by giving us opportunities to trust Him? Typically, these moments happen when we do not want to trust Him or do not understand how to trust Him. In either case, He is asking us to do what we may not be willing to do or do not have the wisdom, insight, clarity, or knowledge to do. When the Lord came upon 5,000 people (not counting the women or the children) who were hungry and needing food, it was not within the disciple's ability to feed them.

> But Jesus said, "They need not go away; you give them something to eat." They told him, "We have only five loaves here and two fish." And he said, "Bring them here to me." Then he ordered the crowds to sit down on the grass, and taking the five loaves and the two fish, he looked up to heaven and said a blessing. Then he broke the loaves and gave them to the disciples, and the disciples gave them to the crowds.
> (Matthew 14:16–19)

At that moment, they were working outside of their collective strengths. At that moment, Jesus had them right where He wanted them. The perfect sweet spot with the Lord is when we have to trust Him rather than ourselves. God calls us to walk by faith, not our strength, cleverness, or insights. The disciples knew there was not enough bread and fish to feed 5,000 people. They were right. There was not enough provision to get the job done. Though they could not see past the bread in their baskets, Jesus could. But the story gets better.

Christ made what the disciples could not make, and He used the disciples to distribute what He made. He stepped up and created when their hands were unable.

How kind of the Lord. He creates what we cannot and chooses to use us despite our complaining and negativity. Can you imagine complaining to the Lord because you have assessed the situation and determined the job is too big, complex, or complicated? Then He comes through by doing the impossible. There have been many instances in my life where I assessed the situation and my abilities and resources to fix the situation and promptly concluded the problems were too big or complicated to repair. Then the Lord did the unexpected. He provided. He accomplished, but He did not stop there.

A Pay Grade Higher

Like the disciples in His day, He allowed me to be part of the process of helping those with whom I was previously lodging my complaints. God wants a relationship with me, but it cannot be what it needs to be until I am willing to trust Him to do what I cannot do. I must genuinely come to the end of myself (Luke 15:17). What about you? Are you in a situation with seemingly no good way out of the mess? I'm asking, are you stuck? Are you working outside your ability, hoping to repair your problems? Working outside of your ability is not a bad thing. Sometimes it is the only right thing. It happens to me every day. I am confronted daily with people and situations that I cannot fix.

Then I realized that changing people is outside the scope of my responsibilities. It is a pay grade well above mine. Being unable to fix people kept me awake at night at the beginning of my counseling career. Then I learned that if I could succeed in the "people fixing business," I would not need God. The Lord kindly reminded me that there was a Savior, and I was not Him. He helped me to repent of my self-reliant thinking while turning to Him for solutions. Today, my job is much simpler than fixing people; I point them to Jesus. Like John the Baptist, I am a signpost. When people come to me for help, I point them to Christ. I have taken up John's mantra, "He must increase, and I must decrease" (John 3:30).

When you come to a place that does not make sense or you cannot figure it out, may I suggest something? How about if you recalibrate your thinking around the gospel? There is nothing like the gospel narrative to bring clarity to our challenges. Imagine standing at the foot of Golgotha on the day they crucified the Savior. The disciples were the same friends who appealed to Christ to take over the Roman world. But there they stood, watching their friend die at the hands of the Romans. It seemed so wrong that He would die. It was all backward to them.

Call to Action

1. Has your life ever seemed backward—going the wrong way?
2. Has it ever seemed to be heading differently from what you expected?

The disciples felt that way on the day their friend died. Watching Christ die pushed them outside the bounds of their human understanding. They wanted, expected, and demanded a king. They were confused, hopeless, angry, and in despair as they saw all their dreams dying on a cross. The most likely candidate to succeed was now bleeding and dying on Adam's tree. They were baffled. Peter had his sword drawn only a few hours earlier and was ready to carve up a victory for Jesus. Now he is looking at King Jesus bleeding to death.

That story is similar to yours: God is always up to something better than you think. It appeared the Romans murdered the Savior, but actually, His Father executed Him (Isaiah 53:10). Why? Because being a king 2,000 years ago was not nearly as good as being a King in eternity. Initially, the disciples did not perceive this assumed "change of plans." Can you look back on your life and thank the Lord that He did not give you the desires of your heart at a time when you were asking for something? I am glad that He did not provide the disciples with their wishes.

Unfortunately, we are uncomfortable not being in the know. We do not like living by faith (Romans 14:23). We want to know the outcomes before we begin. We want to see if it will be okay before we move forward. We want to work within our abilities rather than the Lord's strength. We are no different from the disciples. God is calling you to trust Him—to walk by faith (Matthew 14:31). He will not give you all the answers you desire. If He did explain how it would come to pass, you would return to trusting yourself again. He is calling you to stop trusting yourself. Nothing will clarify this faith tension like the gospel story—of Christ dying on the cross. That story needs to inform your thinking rather than your wits. Whose story are you living?

Will You Give Thanks?

The disciples wanted to live for their story. God had another story in mind. Even when you do not understand what God is doing in your life, it is humble and wise to thank Him with expressions of gratitude for His leadership in your life. Your gratitude does not mean your life will change a lot or at all. Mable's life did not change, but her thoughts about God did. She persistently preached the gospel narrative to herself and experienced a calm soul. Through her ordeal, like the disciples, God brought her to an end of herself. Even though she did not know what He was up to, she decided to trust Him, albeit imperfectly.

If God is holding back from you what you desire, I appeal to you to consider the possibility that He has something better for you. Though He may not give you what you want at this moment, whatever He has planned for you will be far better than you could ever imagine (Ephesians 3:20). The best way to begin this kind of reorientation of the mind is to express gratitude to Him for His sovereign care in your life. Giving thanks is the will of God for you (1 Thessalonians 5:18). Begin right now. Make it your moment-by-moment habit. Perhaps a daily list of things you are thankful for would be a good start. As you do this, will you review what I have shared and answer all my questions in this chapter? You now have your homework assignment.

Beyond Your Ability

9

Comfort Zones

It's easier to trust God when you're in control of things than when you're out of control and unsure of what will happen next. Being in control provides you with a sense of security, confidence, and comfort, albeit it's human-made. The downside to this human-centered worldview is that it's misplaced faith. God calls us to trust Him, not our circumstances. He is the object of our faith, not our preferred outcomes. Because of our loyalty to self-reliance, He may push us beyond our preferences and predictions to teach us to rely on Him.

God for a Day

I can do all things through him who strengthens me.
(Philippians 4:13)

Self-sufficiency is an illusionary lifestyle that puts us at odds with God—to the point that He may have to intervene in our lives to push us beyond our natural abilities. God wants us to put a governor on our desire to control our lives so that we don't think we can function without Him. We forfeited the right to have absolute authority over our lives at regeneration. We surrendered our lives to Him as the supreme ruler. The biblical logic is clear: the Lord can manage things better than we can.

Before Adam sinned, he had no problem relying on God.

He lived with God, loved God, and knew God's love for him. It was a big, beautiful world that Adam lived in, and he enjoyed it. He relied on God alone. There was seemingly nothing he could not do as a God-reliant man. Then the snake entered the Garden and fed Adam a lie through his wife, Eve (Genesis 3:1–6). The snake told Adam he could compete with God by being a god. Adam and Eve believed the lie, creating two possibilities. He could rely on God when necessary and rely on himself too. How cool would it be to be a god for a day, a week, or a lifetime? That was the temptation.

Adam bit the forbidden fruit and got what he wanted: his world was under new management. His eyes opened to see things differently, and running his life was his new vocation. Some things have not changed, have they? Today's culture is without God. They believe they have figured it out. Their internal logic tells them to be all they can be to survive in our big bad world. The mandate is to look out for number one, rely on yourself, and even manipulate others to serve personal agendas. Of course, at some level of their hearts, they know what Adam quickly learned: it's all a lie. Adam could not manage the world in which he lived. People who choose not to trust God will have a similar fearful tension and fate.

> I heard the sound of you in the garden, and I was afraid because I was naked, and I hid myself.
> (Genesis 3:10)

Time to Downsize

Adam soon realized self-reliance was not cracked up to be what he thought it would be. He had to downsize. Living with omnipotence expanded the possibilities to limitless proportions. His choice to walk away from God meant he had to whittle his world down to bite-size pieces because he could not control what God could; he needed something more manageable. Trusting Jehovah did not necessitate a smallish world. Rejecting God to become a god requires thinking small. Being a god was not as easy as Adam thought. Though he used to walk with God in big open places, he now lived in a miniature, defiled version of what things used to be (Psalm 18:19).

Adam chose a world of his own making. It was a microcosm inside of the macrocosm. Knowing that there was something wrong with his new life without God, Adam became afraid. Fear is the typical instigator when we feel a bit out of control. As things continue to escape our ability to manage, we start making excuses for why they are the way they are. Adam's fear motivated him to blame, justify, rationalize, and even escape his surroundings. His cluster of collective sins is common for controllers. Do you recognize Adam's new best friends? Have you ever fallen prey to any of them?

God came to Adam, asking him what he had done, and Adam did not want to be honest by admitting his mistake. God called him out for lying, asking him to trust Him—again. He even provided a means for Adam to do so (Genesis 3:15). God has provided us a means to do this too. His name is Jesus, the Crusher of the serpent's head (John 3:7). We were little gods, regenerated by God, that He called to forego the little worlds of our making. We did this gladly, knowing that becoming a Christian meant relinquishing our rights to God while trusting Him.

Out of Control

All we have to do is give up our rights and accept Him as our God (Romans 10:9). Simple enough, right? Perhaps you have done this. Maybe you have relinquished your rights to being a god and decided to live your life for the true and living God. I hope you have, though there will be continual tension in your relationship with Him. We live in a body that is fallen and quickly lured toward the things of this world (1 John 2:15-16). The daily temptation is to revert to our former manner of life, those comfort zones of being our god where we are in control. Has it ever occurred to you that maybe God sets things up in your life so you can't control them?

Have you ever wondered if God purposely did things to you so you would learn to stop relying on yourself? Parents will do this for their children. They create a controlled context where the child might not succeed, hoping to instill one of his most important lessons; he's not omnipotent. Ceasing from self-trust was God's appeal to Adam. Paul understood this and taught the Corinthians how suffering leads to God-reliance. He knew their tendency because it was his tendency too. He knew that if a person could get away with it, he would reduce his world to something manageable, making themselves god, never relying on anyone, including the Almighty.

> For we do not want you to be ignorant, brothers, of the affliction we experienced in Asia. For we were so utterly burdened beyond our strength that we despaired of life itself. Indeed, we felt that we had received the sentence of death. But that was to make us rely not on ourselves but on God who raises the dead.
> (2 Corinthians 1:8-9)

My Comfort Zone

Paul did not primarily see the trouble that came to him as a negative thing but as God's love. He understood his prideful tendencies and how he needed prodding to break the Adamic struggle of self-reliance. Even though he despaired of life, which is hard to imagine, he realized the merciful love of

God, who wanted Paul to rely on someone more dependable. The diagram in this chapter represents an actual drawing I drew for a couple I was counseling. I hoped to teach them about their sinful tendencies toward self-reliance that killed their marriage. The goal was to point them to their real need—to rely on God, who raises the dead.

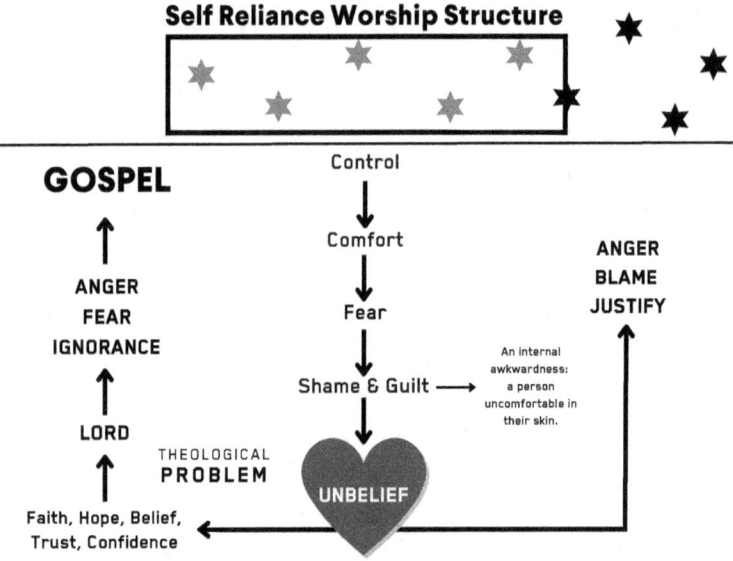

As you see in the picture, they desired to live within their comfort zones—the rectangular box. Inside this box are the things they could do well, nearly ensuring a failure-free life. Each person's comfort zone differs depending on their desires, cravings, dreams, hopes, or expectations. Of course, their strengths and God-given abilities must cooperate with their aspirations. The couple had hoped for a particular life together. As long as circumstances met their expectations as they engineered or manipulated the outcome, it kept them in control, and all was well. The problem with self-sufficient thinking is that it does not require authentic trust in God. It is a little god in charge of a small world—the things inside the box.

Self-reliance is idolatry because people rely on themselves to acquire and control whatever outcome they desire. Self-sufficiency is a worship disorder. God will never allow His children to live with a worship dysfunction. He demands exclusive worship, which is the child of God trusting, relying upon, having confidence, believing, and hoping in Him alone. The Lord could not be more explicit in Exodus 20:3, saying, "You shall have no other gods before me." God will not let us get away with idolatrous thinking and practices. God calls all former little gods—you and me—to trust the true and living God. There is nothing beyond His means that He may choose to use to move us from self-reliance to God-reliance.

Resist and Regret

Paul called it "beyond our strength." If you don't have this kind of God-centered perspective on suffering, you will despair of life, like Paul. You will also be wrestling with the Lord (James 4:6). Typically, the initial sin of a controlling person is the same as the sin of Adam: it is unbelief. You and I sin similarly (Mark 9:24). When our world becomes unwieldy, our first response is not to trust God; other sins like anxiety, worry, or fear follow. You see this in the diagram.

God was moving the couple out of their comfort zone to a place they could not manage, so they would learn to quit relying on themselves and trust Him, who raised the dead. It would be best to trust God when things get out of control—a fantastic response. However, little god controllers typically do what they have habituated themselves into doing most of their lives: they rely on themselves. Self-reliance is their habit; if things get out of control, they default to their practice before trusting God. Of course, their habituation does not work. It creates more dysfunction—personal and relational.

The two most typical ways a person resorts to regain

control of his world are anger and escape. Anger is the most common habit for controllers. It's a manipulative tactic for an insecure person to regain control of the world he feels he is losing. Forms of manipulative anger are anything from rage to the silent treatment, criticism, blaming, justification, and rationalization. Escaping is the dumbing-down habit for controllers. Rather than dealing with the problems, they seek to escape from the problems. Various escapes are alcohol, medication, spending money, video games, TV/movies, and overeating.

Gospel Solution

> *For we do not want you to be unaware, brothers, of the affliction we experienced in Asia. For we were so utterly burdened beyond our strength that we despaired of life itself. Indeed, we felt that we had received the sentence of death. But that was to make us rely not on ourselves but on God who raises the dead.*
>
> (2 Corinthians 1:8–9)

It is interesting how Paul addressed the solution to the problem. He said he learned to trust God, who raises the dead. While you already know what the answer should be—trust God, it is instructive that he would frame the solution in resurrection language. Paul used specific words to communicate the solution. He said they needed to trust the God who raises the dead. He could have said to trust Christ, believe in the cross, hope in the gospel, or any other descriptor that pointed to trusting Almighty God.

He chose the resurrection as how to think about God's ability. He wanted them to know the gospel was more than a man dying on a tree. The gospel is also a man coming out of the grave. He wanted them to think about God's powerful ability in the direst circumstances. Targeting this particular aspect of the gospel is essential for us to understand. You may have a lot of capacity, competency, and courage, but you cannot bring anyone out of the grave. Only God can raise the dead. What He can do for us is far superior to anything we have ever thought about doing for ourselves.

Call to Action

Yes, we can die for someone, but we cannot raise someone from the grave (Romans 5:7). Paul put God in a unique category. Now it's up to us.

1. Will you trust Him? What does it mean to trust God, practically speaking? What is an area of your life that you do not want to yield control?
2. Will you learn how to rely on Him? What would you say if you were to explain to someone what it meant to rely on God? What are the specifics, the steps, and the process?
3. Are there any aspects of self-reliance operative in you? What is your plan for repentance?

One-time repentance will not be enough. Self-reliance is a habituation, a practice. You are going to need help. One of the best things a self-reliant person could do is to humble himself by letting others know about his sin and seek their help. Other reliance is a good start that will help anyone overcome self-reliance.

10

Self-reliance

Self-reliant people live in a self-constructed, self-sustained worship structure that diverts their faith in God to rely on themselves, hoping to engineer pre-determined outcomes. It is not anyone's real world because complete self-sufficiency is an impossible feat to achieve. No finite soul can be totally reliant. Not even Jesus had that ability—in His humanness. God did not create us to be autonomous creatures but to live within a construct of trust and obedience.

Self-Reliance

Jesus grew physically (Luke 2:40, 52). He was tired (John 4:6) and became thirsty (John 19:28). He hungered (Matthew 4:2) and experienced physical weakness (Matthew 4:11; Luke 23:26). Then He died (Luke 23:46). To pursue a self-reliant lifestyle is to push yourself past the boundaries of what Jesus would not dare to do (Luke 22:42). He resisted this temptation by choosing to do something counter-intuitive to self-sufficiency: He humbled Himself to the will of God (John 6:38), always seeking the Father's will, even giving up many hours in prayer to know the purposes and directives of His Father.

> Though he was in the form of God, . . . (He) emptied himself, by taking the form of a servant, being born

> in the likeness of men. And being found in human form, he humbled himself by becoming obedient to the point of death, even death on a cross.
>
> (Philippians 2:6–8)

Self-sufficiency is the self-deceiving and isolating process of trying to be stronger while resisting other people's help, especially help from the Lord. A sinful desire to build a lifestyle and reputation releases a person from trusting someone else. They believe in themselves, whether it's the installation of an Adamic tendency or they have learned through many disappointments not to trust others. Christ resisted this habituating choice. He set aside His glorious reputation and powerful coequality with the Father to become a dependent human being. He embraced human weakness so that He could tap into the strength of the Divine (Luke 22:42; John 6:38).

Though self-reliance and God-reliance are similar in that they promote a person, there is an eternal difference between them. The God-reliant person desires to make God's name great. Self-reliant people crave to make their name great (Daniel 4:30; James 1:14–15). The self-sufficient person presents the oddest of ironies. While their self-reliance projects the image of being strong and in control, they are weak and not in control. Like all humanity, they stand in need of God's empowering grace.

Gospel Irony

Self-reliance is smoke and mirrors. It is a sham. It's a form of insanity to pretend to be something you are not. We are broken and depraved clay pots (Romans 3:23; 2 Corinthians 4:7). We are unable and incapable of accomplishing and sustaining anything outside of God's proactive intervention and provision (1 Corinthians 4:7; Ephesians 2:1–9). We are God-dependent whether we want to admit it or not. The world is clamoring to promote themselves while trying to prove to anyone who will listen how they have it all together because they have tapped into their true selves and achieved their definition of greatness.

> The sacrifices of God are a broken spirit; a broken and contrite heart, O God, you will not despise.
> (Psalm 51:17)

While they try to dress to impress, they are hopeless and bankrupt, frantically resisting humanity's collective death march (Genesis 2:16–17). Real success has never been through self-effort, self-esteem, or self-reliance—three pursuits that lead to competitive individualism. True success begins with a broken and humble posture before the Lord. We find the most profound picture of this gospel irony in the cross of Christ. His death on Adam's tree was God's strength and wisdom profoundly put on display. Listen to how Paul discussed it while instructing the Corinthians about gospel irony.

> For the word of the cross is folly to those who are perishing, but to us who are being saved, it is the power of God.
> (1 Corinthians 1:18)

Personal success is not through might and power (Zechariah 4:6). It is through weakness, as displayed by the humble heart who is willing to submit to God moment by moment, especially when life does not make sense (2 Corinthians 4:7, 12:10).

Self-reliance

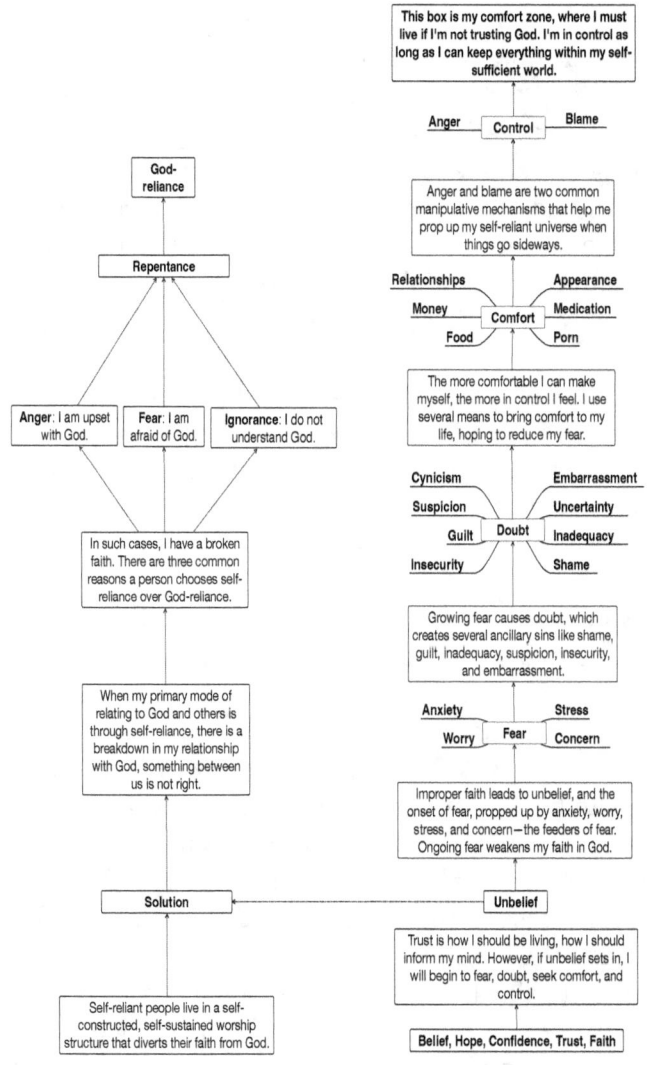

Two Masters

The nature and expectation of self-reliance are to reject God. It is a choice as to whether we want to serve ourselves or serve the Lord. Because Adam continues to reside in us, there is a temptation to choose his dark path over walking in the light. Christians intuitively know that we cannot trust the Lord and ourselves simultaneously. Though Jesus was talking to the Pharisees about money, He laid out a universal truth about the impossibility of simultaneously serving God and man when he said,

> No servant can serve two masters, for either he will hate the one and love the other, or he will be devoted to the one and despise the other. You cannot serve God and money.
> (Luke 16:13)

Because the temptation to be self-reliant is every person's struggle, I developed a mind map to help us better understand the challenges and solutions regarding our universal tension with God. Self-reliance is a dysfunction of the heart that speaks specifically to how we relate to God. He calls us to believe in Him, and because trust is at the heart of the issue, you'll see several synonyms in the bottom right corner of the mind map, like belief, hope, confidence, trust, and faith. These words redundantly convey the significance of trusting the Lord.

I am not using the word trust or belief in a salvific sense, meaning you are not a Christian if you struggle with self-reliance. Self-sufficiency is not the exclusive domain of the unbeliever. Anyone can be an occasional functional atheist even though they are born again. Because it is impossible to trust God perfectly, we must believe and re-believe repeatedly. We must guard our hearts daily while contextualized in a community that encourages and challenges our faith (Hebrews 10:24). If we do not place ourselves in this kind of community, fear will begin to rule our hearts, and our cry will be similar to the gentleman in Mark's Gospel.

> *Immediately the child's father cried out and said, "I believe; help my unbelief!"*
> (Mark 9:24b)

Unbelieving Believer

Adam began to fear when he chose to un-believe in the Garden of Eden. The logic says we will trust someone or something else if we do not trust God. The most common and straightforward option is to trust in ourselves—creating tension because we intuitively know we are not trustworthy. There is always an element of fear when we rely on ourselves. Adam had this self-suspicion when he depended on himself (Genesis 3:8-10). Note the progression in the mind map from a heart of trust to a heart of fear. Most pretending-to-be-strong people have difficulty admitting their fears (2 Corinthians 1:8-9, 4:7, and 12:7-10). Their self-reliant worldview disdains and dismisses fear. They resist this accommodation for what they consider an aberration of the psyche.

Admitting fear goes against their carefully crafted, self-reliant image. Fear on the map is what you find in the self-reliant person's heart. You could draw a heart around the word. Also, note the tributaries of fear—its spiritual feeders: worry, anxiety, stress, and concern. You must feed fear for it to survive, and these four feeders keep fear alive and functioning in the self-reliant heart. The longer fear stays active in the heart, the more the person will be prone to doubt. Doubt is the natural outworking of fear. This fear-to-doubt construct works out in the self-reliant person's behaviors.

For example, he will become afraid or anxious about specific outcomes. Rather than trusting God, he will default to a habituated self-reliant mode to regain control of the situation. One of the most common modes to restore order to a self-controlled, self-perpetuated universe is anger. Anger is a manipulative tactic of the fearful person to regain control of what he believes he's losing. In these anxious moments, he is not sure God will come through for him, so he takes matters into his hands. Though fear and self-reliance appear to be antithetical, as you can see, they are actually in cahoots. Self-reliance does an excellent job of masking a heart of fear.

Hiding Fear

A person will mask fears, doubts, and insecurities in many ways. In the mind map, you will see the word comfort and the ancillary tributaries that feed the desire for comforts, like appearance, money, and relationships. Being a god is hard. Self-reliance is exhausting. The self-reliant person must find rest from running his universe. He does this by seeking means of comfort—a respite from self-centered, kingdom-building work. His go-to comfort cravings depend on the kind of person he is and how he enjoys sin (Hebrews 11:25). Here are a few examples:

- **REPUTATION:** He finds comfort in building his reputation. His self-made greatness feels good. It brings comfort. He can go to nearly inexhaustible lengths to maintain and promote his "I am in control—I am somebody" image.
- **PORNOGRAPHY:** He finds comfort through women, whether on the net, his spouse, or someone else. The porn addict creates a theater for the mind where his women are under his spell. Whenever he needs a self-important booster shot, he can turn to his

woman of choice to feed his ego.
- **ANGER:** He finds comfort by keeping his world in tight-fisted control through anger. He uses passive or aggressive anger as a manipulative tactic to stay in charge. (Caveat: He rarely chooses anger outside of a few close friends because he wants to maintain his reputation. Only his family and associations will typically see his anger.)

Comfort Zone

Because he is not God and cannot rule his universe like God, he has to whittle his world down to something more manageable—something he can control and perpetuate. This smallish universe is his comfort zone. You see it at the top of the mind map. His comfort zone is the place where he enjoys what he has created. He is in control as long as he can keep his life contained in his hermetically sealed universe. Of course, the problem with this worldview is that life is not that neat, contained, or manageable. Life was not meant to be controlled by our self-effort.

God calls us to live by faith in Him, not by faith in ourselves or our abilities (Hebrews 11:6) to keep things under our control. You will quickly discern if you struggle with self-reliance by how you respond when life moves out of your comfort zone. Anything outside the box in the mind map is out of your control. Those moments will force you to make a pivotal decision to trust God or try to regain control of your world according to your preferred outcome. Your responses to life situations will reveal the real motivations of your heart (Luke 6:45)—whether your default is self-reliance or God-reliance.

The self-reliant person will not humble himself to God. He will not experience the redemptive work that only God can do. The self-sufficient soul will exercise whatever means necessary to regain control of his life.

His determination to be self-reliant makes it hard for him to trust others. He struggles to perceive there could be another way of doing things. His native response is to demand, manipulate, and will his way through the difficulty. He has an "I can do all things through me who strengthens me" mentality (Philippians 4:13). He will alienate himself from his friends if he does not repent of his self-reliance, as demonstrated by building community. The self-reliant soul promotes individualism, perpetuating disunity, dividing people, hurting feelings, creating misunderstandings, and instilling relational dysfunction.

Call to Action

Self-reliance is a crisis of faith. The cure brings us back to the gospel. If you struggle with self-reliance, as I do, you must relearn how to re-believe. Self-reliance is a loud and proud declaration that God is insufficient to care for your life. You may be a believer in that you have been born a second time (John 3:7), but you are not entirely trusting the Lord in your sanctification. Here are a few questions that will assist you in thinking about how to change.

1. What is a circumstance that tempts you to rely on yourself? For most of us, it will be a recurring fear of something happening in our lives.
2. What do you think is motivating you to take matters into your hands? Are you reacting to childhood shaping influences? Is it just how you have always been? Why are you motivated this way?
3. Will you articulate why you are this way? If you can write down or discuss with someone why you are this way, it will bring clarity in processing what's wrong.
4. What is it about God that tempts you to not rely on Him? There are three answers to this question;

typically, it combines all three. "I won't trust God because I'm afraid of, angry with, or don't completely understand Him."
5. Will you find a friend who will walk with you through this journey? The solution is to restore this gospel dysfunction of the heart. It will not auto correct. You must explore and repair the brokenness. With whom will you share this information.

Final Thought:

I have asked you many questions throughout this book. The best use of it and the most beneficial for you is carefully working through each question with a friend. You're not in a hurry; you know the analogy: the Christian life is a marathon, not a sprint. Find your friend. Talk to them about what you just read. Ask them to walk with you as you reread and seek to apply.

Also, please take advantage of our website, where you will find thousands of free resources to help you fight the good fight of boasting in God's strength through our weaknesses.

About the Author

Rick Thomas launched the Life Over Coffee global training network in 2008 to bring hope and help for you and others by creating resources that spark conversations for transformation. His primary responsibilities are resource creation and leadership development, which he does through speaking, writing, podcasting, and educating. In 1990 he earned a BA in Theology and, in 1991, a BS in Education. In 1993, he received his ordination into Christian ministry, and in 2000, he graduated with an MA in Counseling from The Master's University. In 2006, he was recognized as a Fellow of the Association of Certified Biblical Counselors (ACBC).

Other Books Available from Life Over Coffee

Boasting in Weakness
Centering Your Marriage on Christ
Communication
Complete Marriage
Don't Apologize
Exchange the Truth for a Lie
Help My Marriage Has Grown Cold
Identity Crisis
Local Church
Loving Me
Mad
Marriage Devotion We Are One
Politics and Culture
Parenting Devotion from Zero to Adulthood
Sex, Temptation, and Modesty
Storm Hurler
The Cyber Effect
The Talk
Wives Leading
You Decide